# STRENGTH TRAINING
# FOR TRIATHLETES

# STRENGTH TRAINING

## FOR

## TRIATHLETES

PATRICK HAGERMAN, EdD

BOULDER, COLORADO

Disclaimer:
Before embarking on any strenuous exercise program, including the training described in this book, everyone, particularly anyone with a known heart or blood-pressure problem, should be examined by a physician.

VeloPress®, a division of Competitor Group, Inc.
1830 North 55th Street
Boulder, Colorado  80301-2700 USA
303/440-0601; Fax: 303/444-6788; E-mail: velopress@competitorgroup.com

To purchase additional copies of this book or other VeloPress books, call 800/234-8356 or visit us on the Web at velopress.com.

Distributed in the United States and Canada by Publishers Group West

Cover photo by Don Karle
Cover design by Judith Stagnitto Abbate / Abbate Design
Interior design by Erin Johnson / Erin Johnson Design
Illustrations by Tom Ward

Library of Congress Cataloging-in-Publication Data

Hagerman, Patrick S.
  Strength training for triathletes / Patrick Hagerman.
      p. cm.
  ISBN 978-1-934030-15-8 (alk. paper)
  1.  Triathlon—Training. 2.  Physical fitness.  I. Title.
  GV1060.73.H34 2008
  796.42'57—dc22

                              2008018542

Printed in China / Asia Pacific Offset
08   09   10   /   10   9   8   7   6   5   4   3   2   1

# Contents

# PART I

# Strength Training Program Components

# 1

# Strength Training Versus Endurance Training

Triathlon is an endurance sport, plain and simple. So why should you consider strength training a necessary part of a triathlon workout? The answer is simple, but it takes a complex explanation to put it all together. The short explanation is that strength training makes muscles stronger, and stronger muscles can perform longer at higher intensities before they fatigue. The long version breaks down what is really happening during strength training and endurance training and examines the subtle differences and similarities. This book takes the long route because understanding how the body works makes it much easier to plan training programs so that they work to your advantage.

## DEFINING STRENGTH AND ENDURANCE TRAINING

If you ask any triathlete what endurance training is, the most common answer has something to do with swimming, running, or cycling. Technically, *endurance training* is any type of exercise that is rhythmical, maintains an increased heart rate and oxygen consumption, and uses large muscle groups to propel the body. It is also referred to as *aerobic* training because the body relies on a continuous, increased supply of oxygen during the energy-making processes at the cellular level. This supply of oxygen comes from increased respiration, usually the result of taking deeper breaths and breathing more frequently. In addition to increased respiration, the heart must pump more blood to the muscles to deliver the oxygen. So there is an increase in heart rate and respiration that is maintained during the entire exercise bout: That's endurance training.

Ask the same triathlete what strength training is, and the answer usually involves some sort of weight lifting. In the most literal sense, *strength training* can be any type of training that increases the endurance, size, power, or strength of the specific muscles being used, regardless of what type of exercise is being done or whether there is actually any "pumping iron" going on. Strength training is done in short bouts, with rest periods interspersed throughout the workout; is not rhythmical; and involves many different muscle groups, some large and some small. Strength training is considered *anaerobic*, or without oxygen, even though you are still breathing and your body is delivering oxygen to the muscles, because the processes that provide energy for strength training do not rely on oxygen as the aerobic processes do.

Another difference between strength and endurance training is that the former does not improve the cardiovascular system to any great extent. Your heart is still beating, but strength training is typically performed in short bursts that don't require large increases in blood flow from the heart. During endurance training, as the heart rate increases, the amount of work the heart does increases, so the heart muscle must be able to keep up the pace. To do this, the cardiac muscle tissue gets stronger, and the heart becomes more efficient at pumping blood. During strength training, large, sustained increases in heart rate don't occur, and increases in oxygen delivery to the muscles are not needed, so the heart doesn't have to become stronger or more efficient.

The energy systems involved in endurance and strength training also differ in what they use as fuel. Along with delivering oxygen to muscles, the blood carries glucose (blood sugar) to the working muscles. During endurance training, glucose is broken down to provide a majority of the energy you use and allows you to burn fat stores. Glucose is not stored in muscles in large enough quantities to sustain exercise for very long, so delivery via the blood from a pumping heart is required. In strength training the body does not need to break down glucose for energy; it uses the stored glycogen in the muscles. Energy delivery during strength training has to be done very fast, so the immediate stores of glycogen are a better option than glucose.

If we think of our bodies as weight, we are lifting weight all the time during a triathlon or endurance training.

Anatomically, there is a great difference between strength and endurance training, but there are also some gray areas where the two overlap. Think about how often you lift weights during a triathlon. Other than lifting a cup of water to your mouth, your bike off the rack, and maybe yourself off the ground, you don't lift that much—or do you? When you stop thinking of weights as made of iron and attached to a barbell or machine, you realize that your body is a weight that you have to lift and move all the time—and your muscles have to move it. When you run, your legs have to push and hold up your entire body weight. When you swim, your arms help to pull your body through the resistance of the water. When you cycle, your arms support your upper body as your legs push against the forces of the bike and pedals to propel you forward. So if we think of our bodies as weight, we are lifting weight all the time during a triathlon or endurance training. It may not seem like much weight, but over the course of an endurance training session your muscles become fatigued from all that lifting, and your heart gets tired from all that pumping.

To produce improvement in any type of training program, there has to be an overload, and the only way to provide it is first to make your body carry that weight in longer training sessions.

If strength training makes our muscles stronger, then it makes sense that swimming, running, and cycling make our muscles stronger because we are working with the weight of our bodies. The weight is just a mass of muscle and bones rather than iron plates. Ask yourself, Have my muscles gotten stronger after a swimming, running, or cycling program? If the answer is yes, then congratulations, you have been doing a form of strength training all along and didn't even know it.

The next question should be, If I am already doing a strength training program with my body weight, and that's all that I really lift during a triathlon, why should I start a strength training program that uses free weights or machines? Some triathletes will answer that question with, "I don't have to, what I do is good enough." If what you have been doing were good enough to bring you the performances you want, you probably wouldn't be reading this book.

The problem with relying on your body weight to increase strength during endurance training is that your weight is not enough of a stimulus because your body is already used to it. To produce improvement in any type of training program, there has to be an overload, and the only way to provide it is first to make your body carry that weight in longer training sessions. But longer training sessions aren't enough to improve your performance and speed for shorter distances, so you next have to add external weight in a manner the body is not used to; that's how you create the correct stimulus.

Here's an analogy that may better explain this concept. Say you have a really large SUV, but it came with a lawnmower engine, so it doesn't go very fast or have much power. You take it to the repair shop, and they replace the lawnmower engine with a big, strong V8 engine. Now you can speed along as fast as you like and have plenty of power to pass slower cars. Your body is just like the SUV. If you keep the same body, but change the engine that moves it so that it's stronger and has more power, then your athletic performances will improve. This is what strength training does, and it does so differently than endurance training.

Obviously the mechanics of a conventional strength training program using some form of free weights or machines are quite different from those of conventional endurance training that triathletes use (swimming, running, and cycling). The type of strength training you need is all about lifting weights, but in a way that directly benefits your swimming, running, and cycling. This is called sport-specific strength training. It mimics the movements of the sport, uses the same muscles used in the sport, and is applied in such a way that the intensity benefits the sport. Strength training for triathletes isn't a matter of just going to the gym and using whatever machine you come across; it has to be done in a deliberate and efficient way for you to get the most out of your efforts.

Four possible physiological outcomes can be achieved through a strength training program. A *physiological outcome* is the way the body changes, in this case how your muscles change. The four results are

- increased muscular endurance,
- muscular hypertrophy,
- increased muscular power, and
- increased muscular strength.

## SAID PRINCIPLE

Specific Adaptations to Imposed Demands is the basis for sport-specific strength training. This means that your body will adapt in a very specific way based on the demands that you impose on it during training. For example, to make your arms stronger you have to train your arms, not your legs; or in endurance terms, to become a better swimmer, you have to swim, not run.

How you achieve each of these outcomes is covered in Chapter 2, but for now you need to understand how these outcomes are different.

*Muscular endurance* is the ability of a muscle to withstand repeated use over a period of time. *Muscular hypertrophy* is an increase in muscle mass or size. *Muscular power* is the ability to move the body quickly through the use of very fast muscular contractions. *Muscular strength* is the amount of "weight" that the muscles can move in a single effort. Each of these outcomes has a place in a triathlete's training program. The key is to achieve just the right amount of each outcome at just the right time. It's very important to remember that strength training doesn't necessarily mean your muscles will get bigger. Far too often I hear the excuse, "I don't want to lift weights because that will make my muscles too big." That's just plain wrong. Increased size is only one outcome, and you don't have to focus on it if you don't need to.

## HOW STRENGTH TRAINING FOR TRIATHLETES IS DIFFERENT

As you've just discovered, all strength training routines are not the same. In fact, a sport-specific strength training program for one triathlete can be different from another triathlete's. It all depends on the level of training a particular person needs and the length of the triathlon he or she is training for. But even more important, strength training for triathletes should be very different from programs used by bodybuilders, powerlifters, and the general public. Everyone has the same muscles and bones, but how they are used can be different. Training goals, or outcomes, determine the use and are reached by using different combinations of exercises, sets, reps, rest periods, exercise order, weight, and progression plans.

For example, a bodybuilder is interested in one thing: size. The bigger the better in this case. Having large, bulging muscles is not what a triathlete wants, because body mass negatively affects endurance efficiency, and larger muscles add a lot of mass but not necessarily a lot of strength. The bigger your muscles are, the more mass you have and the more strength it takes to move that mass, especially over a long distance. Mass also creates resistance in the water and frontal air resistance on land. Many people assume that bodybuilders are proportionately strong. But having large muscles and having strong muscles are not always the same thing. To bodybuilders, size is more important than strength, and although they can move a lot of weight, many athletes are both smaller and stronger.

The triathlete can benefit from larger muscles if that increased size is kept in check and is used properly. If you want to increase the performance of a muscle, sometimes you have to start by increasing its size, because you can't make a muscle better if you don't have enough muscle to begin with. Once the muscle size is where it needs to be, changing the strength training emphasis will change the outcome and keep you moving in the right direction. A muscle that is the right size can be made stronger and more powerful or be given more endurance. So don't rule out using a strength training program that focuses on hypertrophy, because there are times when it will be necessary.

Powerlifting is another sport that uses strength training differently than triathlon does. Powerlifters who compete in contests for bench press, squat, and deadlift, as well as weightlifters who compete in the Olympic lifts of the snatch and clean-and-jerk, are usually very strong for their size. This is the complete opposite of bodybuilders, and more in line with what triathletes need. In these sports, success has everything to do with how much you can lift and nothing to do with how big you look. Some of the strongest lifters pound for pound are actually women. What makes a powerlifting or weightlifting athlete's workout different from what a triathlete needs is the types of exercises used and the reps, sets, and weight used. These heavyweight sports have almost no endurance component at all because a competitive lift consists of one repetition that will last anywhere from 2 to 20 seconds. A triathlete needs the compact, strong muscles but requires much more endurance from them.

General fitness programs are likewise not useful for triathletes, mainly because of their wide range of variety and lack of sport-specific exercises. Training for general fitness is more about working all the different parts of the body in a manner designed to work as many muscles at one time as possible, often using machines that are designed to make the exercise comfortable rather than to mimic a sport movement. For example, several popular exercises that strengthen

## ENDURANCE EFFICIENCY

Endurance efficiency is the amount of energy you use per pound of body weight during aerobic training. The goal for triathletes is to be very efficient by having lean, strong muscles, not large, weak muscles.

the chest, such as the bench press, seated chest press, and fly, have nothing to do with triathlon. So although most of the exercise programs you find in popular magazines will improve your fitness, they won't do much to improve your triathlon performance. The key is to choose exercises that mimic the sport of triathlon and put them together in a way that works just for you.

## THE EFFECTS OF STRENGTH TRAINING

Several performance components affected by strength training can boost your triathlon results. The first component is muscular power. *Power* is the ability to produce force quickly. In a triathlon this is useful during short sprints, uphill cycling, and transitioning into and out of the water. A powerful muscle is able to call upon its anaerobic energy stores to provide for quick movement. Strength training increases muscular power in two ways: The more muscle you have, the less effort it takes to produce a given amount of power (remember the SUV analogy), and strength training trains your muscles to reproduce energy quickly so they don't tire as fast and can recover from short bouts of high-intensity movement. Energy production is achieved deep down in the muscle fibers, where the stores of glycogen (the storage form of glucose), enzymes that increase the speed of muscular contraction, and stored creatine and phosphocreatine (energy substrates) are all increased because of strength training.

The second component is that you can increase your speed in every event through strength training. This is the result of the selective recruitment of fast-twitch muscle fibers during strength training. During endurance training you mainly use your slow-twitch fibers, which are designed for low power output and long-term use. During strength training you have to call upon the fast-twitch muscle fibers for their high power and force output. The downside to fast-twitch fibers is that they fatigue very quickly—usually in less than five minutes. When you are endurance training and decide to put on a burst of speed, you know that it won't last very long and that you'll have to slow back down to your regular pace. Strength training builds up the ability of the fast-twitch muscle fibers to activate and provide that burst of speed. You will still have to slow back down, but you can obtain a higher-intensity burst of speed (meaning faster) that you will recover from faster, so you can do it again when you need to.

The third component that strength training improves has an indirect effect on your immediate performance: a reduction in body fat because of an increase in lean mass. Decreasing one's body fat is typically equated with losing fat, but the equation has two sides—you can also increase lean tissue. Endurance training burns a lot of fat, but doesn't build much lean tissue. Strength training is all about increasing lean tissue. Again, we are not talking about bodybuilder-size muscles, but about making the muscles you have more dense. Increasing muscle density brings down your fat-to-lean ratio, which equals improved performance because fat doesn't assist in movement—all it does is sit there, needing muscle to move it along. Increased lean tissue means more muscle to produce movement, which is exactly what you want, because muscle essentially carries itself—it isn't a freeloader like fat.

When you have more muscle to draw from, it takes longer to wear it out.

Finally, increasing muscular strength increases muscular endurance. When you have more muscle to draw from, it takes longer to wear it out. If you find that you sometimes reach muscular fatigue before you reach cardiovascular fatigue, then you should increase your muscular strength so that you have more in reserve. Endurance training decreases cardiovascular fatigue; strength training increases muscular endurance, which in turn decreases muscular fatigue.

## TRAINING FOR DIFFERENT DISTANCES

Not all strength training programs for triathletes are alike, even though they employ similar exercises. Applied to triathlon, strength training will differ depending on the triathlon distance you are training for. Performing well in a shorter sprint race relies more on speed and power than muscular endurance, whereas an Iron-distance event requires less speed and power and more muscular endurance. In the middle you have the Olympic and half-Iron distances, which are a combination of speed and endurance. So different distances will require strength training programs with different outcomes. The balance of each outcome with the training distance is probably the most important aspect of program design. Think of it like this: You can't train like a bodybuilder would and expect to perform well in a triathlon—it's not going to work! The distance you strive for will affect the reps, sets, and weights you use (more on this in Chapter 2), as well as how often you can train in combination with your endurance training schedule. It all has to come together in just the right way for it to work. After an explanation of the specific components, later chapters provide more detailed information on putting together a program for each specific distance.

## TIME VERSUS BENEFITS

If you have been a triathlete for some time, you know how many hours you need to put into your endurance training. At times it may seem as though you're doing endless laps in the pool, thousands of mind-numbing pedal strokes, and boring miles on the road. At the end of all this you may be thinking that you don't have time for strength training—there are only so many hours in a day, after all. Fortunately, strength training doesn't take very much time. If you can spare 30 minutes a day, 3 days a week, the results you will get will make you want to do more. It's even possible to cut back your endurance training to make room for strength training and end up with better endurance training sessions.

If you could spend 90 minutes a week increasing your body's ability to perform during all those other hours you train, wouldn't it be worth it? Of course it would! Your runs will become faster, your strokes more powerful, and your spinning quicker—all without a mindful increase in effort. That's the beauty of strength training: Not only do you feel stronger, but everything else improves as a result. And this happens very quickly. Your body will respond to a strength training program within the first couple of weeks. You probably won't notice much in the mirror (this isn't bodybuilding) because the changes will be happening on the inside first. As I mentioned before, you need to find the right combination of muscle density and efficiency.

It is also possible to do too much strength training. The additional strain that strength training adds to your entire program can be too much if you don't ease into it and back off on your endurance training at the same time. This situation is called overtraining, and it will set back your performance, extend the time it takes you to recover from injuries, and just plain slow you down. Nothing is worse than a muscle that won't heal because you push it too far. A proper strength training program must be put together with your entire training regimen in mind and without pushing your body too far. This book provides some guidelines to get you started in the right direction, but ultimately you need to listen to how your body responds and let it guide you toward the proper balance of strength and endurance training for you.

## INTENSITY OF TRAINING

Probably the most important component of your strength training program is the intensity, which is a combination of the weights you use, how much you rest between sets, and the length of a workout. To properly produce the efficiency you want, and to push the muscular endurance levels upward, the intensity has to be set so that you are constantly moving from one exercise to another, with just enough rest between each set of an exercise to allow for enough energy recuperation, but not so much that you cool down before you start up again. The best way to do this is to group exercises together in repeating series called circuits. This is an advanced version of the circuit training programs that were popular during the 1980s, but with much more science added in to make it actually work.

How much weight you can move isn't the key to intensity; it's putting the right amount of resistance in the right place during the right movement.

Intensity is not just about how much weight you can lift. In fact, in many exercises the weight is just your body weight or just a few extra pounds. How much weight you can move isn't the key to intensity; it's putting the right amount of resistance in the right place during the right movement. It all has to fit in with triathlon movements and the muscles used in some specific way. Intensity changes during a triathlon, and it changes during a strength training session. As you learn the components of a good program and see how to put together a program just for you, you will learn how intensity can be manipulated to your benefit.

# PRINCIPLE OF SPECIFICITY

Specificity is one of the most important concepts behind strength train-ing for sports. As I mentioned previously, sport strength training has to be designed to mimic the sport you are training for. For example, if you wanted to enter a bench press competition, you would spend a lot of time doing the bench press. In triathlon, you aren't lifting any specific weights, but the movements you produce during the swim, bike, and run can be mimicked in a weight room with a little creativ-ity. Unfortunately equipment manufacturers haven't produced a lot of triathlon-specific exercise machines, so many of the exercises in this book take a little imagination to do, but they are all part of the bigger movements involved in our sport. As an example, a squat will definitely make your legs stronger, but when in a triathlon are you pushing off with both feet at the same time? Never! However, during cycling you extend the hip, knee, and ankle of one leg at a time, over and over. So all you have to do is develop an exercise that allows you to mimic this "one-leg squat" to create a sport-specific exercise. Keep this in mind as you flip through the book and try the exercises in Part III; they may still look silly, but you'll know why they work.

# 2

# By the Numbers:
# Reps, Sets, Weight, and Rest

**N**ow that you have established that a strength training program is what you need, the next step is building your program based on sound scientific evidence. There are many strength training programs available, but they aren't all designed for triathlon goals, and unfortunately many of them just don't deliver the goods. A solid training program should be based on scientific evidence rather than on what the guy on the next treadmill is doing. The same goes for copying the training program of a successful athlete. Just because a training program produced results for another person doesn't mean it will do the same for you. How much your body changes with any training program will be determined by your genes. However, if you are using the most scientifically sound program available, one developed for your goals and strengths, you can take full advantage of what your parents gave you. This chapter is all about numbers—and in strength training, there are lots of numbers. Choosing the correct number of repetitions per set, the right number of sets, and the perfect amount of weight for each exercise, as well as resting just enough, are key to getting the results you want.

# DIFFERENT REPS FOR DIFFERENT GOALS

The number of repetitions you complete in each set of an exercise greatly influences the result of that exercise. As discussed in Chapter 1, the 4 main physiological results that can be achieved with strength training are muscular endurance, hypertrophy, power, and strength. This list shows the corresponding number of repetitions per set to achieve each goal:

- Muscular endurance = 12–20 reps
- Hypertrophy = 6–12 reps
- Power or strength = 1–6 reps

There is some overlap in the number of repetitions from one goal to the next. There are two reasons for this. First, when you train for one goal, you automatically receive a small amount of the benefits from each of the others. For example, if you train for strength, you will also become slightly more powerful, increase muscle mass a little bit, and have more muscular endurance. The key here is that you will change the most in the main goal. If you train for strength, you will become stronger than if you trained for muscular endurance, and vice versa. This is called the *carryover effect*.

Second, science has not yet determined the optimum number of repetitions for each goal. Since the first research on strength training was published 60 years ago, these numbers have become more precise, and in another 10 years they will likely change more. Over time, the picture becomes clearer.

The range of repetitions for each goal also gives you some room to work and progress (more on progression in Chapter 3). Having a range of repetitions is always better than having a single, preset number, allowing for normal day-to-day variations in training. Some days you may be feeling great, so you will do extra reps. Other days you aren't at the top of your game, so you will do fewer reps. Your program can handle these fluctuations, so as long as you stay within the range of repetitions for your goal, you'll stay on track.

In popular magazines that publish training programs, 10 reps always seems to be the "magic number." However, there are no magic numbers in exercise science. Because most of those training programs use 10 repetitions per set, they are actually about making muscles bigger (10 reps is right in the middle of hypertrophy). Because a triathlete should not always be focusing on bigger muscles, you should disregard many of the training programs available to the public. Depending on the specific goal for your triathlon-based strength training program, the number of repetitions you do for each set is straightforward.

## SINGLE VERSUS MULTIPLE SETS

There is an ongoing argument over whether to use a single set for each exercise or multiple sets per exercise, based on the fact that if you are doing nothing, 1 set per exercise will provide noticeable benefits. However, this argument doesn't apply to athletes, because you are considered "trained," already involved in an exercise program of some sort. For athletes, 1 set has clearly been shown to be inferior to multiple sets, but the exact number of sets you need has not been defined. What scientific research has shown is that for each goal there is a range of sets that provides the most benefit:

- Muscular endurance = 2–3 sets
- Hypertrophy = 3–5 sets
- Power or strength = 3–6 sets

Again, there is an overlapping number, in this case 3. There are fewer sets to complete for muscular endurance compared with strength, power, and hypertrophy. There is a somewhat inverse relationship between the number of repetitions for each goal and the number of sets you complete. On the muscular endurance end, you are doing the most reps but the smallest number of sets. On the power and strength end, you are doing the fewest reps but the most sets. This is all a function of exercise *volume,* which is the total amount of weight you lift during an exercise or workout. It is calculated by multiplying sets times reps times weight. Setting weight aside, a balance is created by adjusting the levels of sets and reps. As one goes up, the other goes down. This helps to keep the volume of exercise you do fairly even over time and goals.

Another reason that the number of sets goes down as reps go up is to prevent overuse injuries. Even with a relatively light weight, doing repetition after repetition will eventually wear on your joints. To prevent this, the number of sets is adjusted downward. As the weight gets heavier and you do fewer reps, there is less chance of repetitive motion injury, but you will need to do more sets to give your body enough stimulus to improve.

## CHOOSING THE RIGHT WEIGHT

The question I am asked most often is, how much weight should I be using? Unfortunately, this is the most difficult question to answer because everyone has different capabilities. It is impossible to tell exactly how much weight you should use on every exercise unless you are tested on every exercise. This is where you will have to do some work to set up your own program. Reps and sets are universal numbers; weight is not. However, the method for determining how much weight to use is the same for everyone. It involves testing to determine your estimated 1-rep maximum, or 1RM (the maximum amount of weight you could lift 1 time with correct form). This testing requires trial and error, but the method is straightforward. Once you have your estimated 1RM, you can use a percentage of that (percent 1RM) to set your training goal.

Researchers have been working on finding the most appropriate percent 1RM for each training goal but have yet to discover the best number, so we have ranges of resistance:

- Muscular endurance = 50–67% 1RM

- Hypertrophy = 67–85% 1RM

- Power or strength = 85–100% 1RM

Again, there is some overlap, for the same reasons that repetitions overlap. The most important point is that the amount of weight you use increases as you move from muscular endurance to hypertrophy to power or strength. This fits perfectly into our understanding of muscular endurance, which is about lifting a "lighter" weight numerous times, versus strength, which is about lifting a "heavier" weight a few times.

The number of reps you complete in any given set is inversely proportional to the weight you use. Put simply, the more something weighs, the fewer times you can lift it; the lighter it is, the more times you can lift it. So depending on your goal, not only will your reps change, but so will the weight you'll be using. Table 2.1 lists approximately how much weight you can lift (as a percentage of your 1-rep maximum) for a given number of repetitions.

| TABLE 2.1 | Repetitions and percentage of 1-rep max weight possible | | |
|---|---|---|---|
| 1 | rep | = | 100% |
| 2 | reps | = | 95% |
| 3 | reps | = | 93% |
| 4 | reps | = | 90% |
| 5 | reps | = | 87% |
| 6 | reps | = | 85% |
| 7 | reps | = | 83% |
| 8 | reps | = | 80% |
| 9 | reps | = | 77% |
| 10 | reps | = | 75% |
| 11 | reps | = | 70% |
| 12 | reps | = | 67% |

## Estimating Your 1-Rep Max

To make this book applicable to everyone, instead of using actual weights in our program designs, we use percentages of your 1-rep max to describe how much weight to use in any given exercise. This does not apply to exercises that use only your body weight for resistance, because you can't use just a percentage of your weight; you have to use it all. With any exercise that uses external weight for added resistance (squats, biceps curls, etc.), using percent 1RM allows you to put together a program based on your goals and then plug in the actual weights you will use on each exercise later. It also allows you to swap exercises in and out of your program without changing the goal of the program—so long as you keep using the appropriate percent 1RM.

The downside to using percent 1RM is that you have to figure out what your 1RM is for each exercise. There are 2 ways to go about this: (1) Actually do a maximum lift test for every exercise, or (2) complete a submaximal lift for each exercise and estimate 1RM from that. Testing your 1RM on each exercise can be very tiring, and if you aren't skilled in an exercise, it can cause acute injury that will delay your training. Using a submaximal lift and calculating your 1RM from that gives you a very close estimate without so much effort and risk of injury. This calculation isn't perfect, but it's close enough (usually within a few pounds) for your needs.

The couple of workouts you spend testing will be more than worth the effort later. For each exercise, find a weight that you can lift 3 to 10 times. If you can do 11 reps, increase the weight and try it again after a short rest. It doesn't matter if you can do only 3 reps, 7 reps, or 10 reps—as long as the number is from 3 to 10 you can calculate your 1RM by multiplying the weight you use by the corresponding rep factor (see Table 2.2). For example, on the front raise exercise you completed a test of 8 reps with 20 pounds. Using Table 2.2, multiply

20 pounds by the rep factor for 8 reps (1.27) to get an estimated 1RM of 25.4 pounds (20 × 1.27). It's not uncommon to end up with an estimate that includes a decimal point; you will deal with that later.

The next step involves calculating the amount of weight you actually want to use. Continuing with the same example, if your estimated 1RM is 25.4 pounds, and you choose to start with 65 percent 1RM (training for muscular endurance), multiply the estimated 1RM by the percentage you want to use. In this case, 65 percent of 25.4 pounds is 16.51 pounds. The weights you find in the gym come in only whole numbers, and usually only in increments of 2.5 or 5 pounds, so you have to round the decimal number. For this example, you would round 16.51 down to 15 pounds. Always round down rather than up, because it's better to add weight later than to use too much and have to take it back off.

These calculations come to roughly 65 percent of the 1RM for that particular exercise. Again, this isn't perfect, but it's close enough, and you will make refinements later to get it even closer. Repeat this procedure for all the other exercises in your program. This will take some time, and you may have to adjust the trial weight several times until you find the right weight, but don't rush it. It's better to take your time and get this right.

Finally, retesting your 1RM at regular intervals is an important part of keeping your training program on track. As you train, your body adapts and becomes stronger, which means your 1RM will go up. This occurs no matter what goal you are training for, but it will happen faster if you are training for strength. Retest your 1RM about every 3 months and adjust the weights you are using to keep your program within the correct ranges for your goal. Three-month intervals should be long enough to show sufficient improvement to make the time spent testing and recalculating worthwhile. Doing it more frequently would use up training time to make very small changes that won't make much difference in the weights you use.

### Effects of Your Body Weight

So what about all the exercises that don't obviously involve weight? Remember that your body weight *is* weight; it *is* resistance that your muscles are working against. When you do a body weight exercise, you have to lift your entire weight, or at least the weight of the part of your body that is moving. Because you can't lift a percentage of your body weight, you can't make pull-ups or push-ups any easier unless you lose weight or get stronger. Most body weight exercises are shuffled into the category of muscular endurance training (provided that you can complete at least 12 of them). It is possible to increase the resistance of body weight exercises, such as by adding ankle or wrist weights or wearing a weighted vest. But this turns them into weighted exercises instead of body weight exercises (specific ways to increase the resistance of body weight exercises are discussed in later chapters). You don't have to calculate an estimated 1RM for these exercises because the weight is still your body weight plus a small amount; just stick with the correct number of reps for your goal.

## GETTING ENOUGH REST

It has been said that rest is the most important part of any training program. The improvements we see don't come about during training; they happen during the rest or recovery period in between training. That's when your body responds to the training and adapts to it in preparation for the next session. That being said, most serious triathletes engage in endurance training almost every day. Fortunately the body responds very well to daily training, as long as you have built up to this point slowly and know exactly how hard you can push yourself. The key to recovering from endurance training lies in its relatively low intensity spread out over the training session. It's easy for the body to recover from exercise that uses large muscle groups and doesn't stress any one system too much.

The improvements we see don't come about during training; they happen during the rest or recovery period in between training.

Strength training is a little different. Instead of working large groups of muscles, you may be focusing on individual muscle areas, single joints, and heavier loads over a number of repetitions and sets. This requires a different approach to rest.

## Rest Between Sets

Getting the proper amount of rest between sets is important in de-signing a strength workout. To allow the anaerobic energy systems to recover enough to complete the next set, you have to rest just enough but not too much. There are several methods for determining the proper amount of rest, most based on subjective feelings rather than science. Some people rest enough between sets to allow their heart rate to return to resting, some people let their breathing return to normal, and others like to have a cup of coffee or a nap between sets. According to the research, the amount of rest should be based on how fast your anaerobic energy systems recover. The key is not to allow your body to fully recover; let it recover just enough, so that the next set will be slightly more fatiguing. Making your body work with an incomplete recovery forces it to adapt. If you wait until you are totally recovered, your body will not have to get any better because it will be allowed to work within its capabilities. In general, it takes about 7 minutes to replenish 90 percent of your ATP (the energy that the anaerobic systems produce). In 3 minutes, only about 50 percent of your ATP has been restocked. The strength training programs you will be doing won't totally deplete your ATP, so you don't have to wait this long between sets. That would make for a really long workout!

The amount of rest between sets that you need depends on your goal. Here's the breakdown:

- Muscular endurance = less than 30 seconds
- Hypertrophy = 30–90 seconds
- Power or strength = 1.5–3 minutes

## ATP

Adenosine triphosphate is the form of energy that your body uses to produce muscular contractions. Every form of food you eat (carbohydrates, fat, and protein), and the substrates it is converted to in the body (glucose, glycogen), is eventually broken down to make ATP. This is the only source of energy your body can use for movement.

The amount of rest is directly linked to the amount of energy provided by the anaerobic energy systems and the intensity of the exercise. For muscular endurance training, very little rest is needed because the intensity is low (60 to 67 percent 1RM), and the goal is to keep your muscles working as much as possible. In hypertrophy training you need a little longer between sets because the intensity is higher (67 to 85 percent 1RM). Finally, in power or strength training the low number of reps and the higher intensity (85 to 100 percent 1RM) require the most rest between sets. Don't let this lead you to believe that a power or strength workout will take a long time, though, because that isn't true. To allow enough rest between sets but not make your workout too long, stack your exercises in a circuit so that you are actually completing a set of a different exercise, using different muscles, while you are resting from the last set. So while one muscle is resting, you are working another. You may have to stack 2 to 3 exercises in a circuit to allow enough time between sets for power or strength training, and you may choose not to stack any for muscular endurance training. See Table 2.3 for a review of all the component ranges.

| TABLE 2.3 | Repetition, set, weight, and rest guidelines | | |
|---|---|---|---|
| | Muscular Endurance | Hypertrophy | Power or Strength |
| Training Goal Repetitions | 12–20 | 6–12 | 1–6 |
| Sets | 2–3 | 3–5 | 3–6 |
| Weight | 50–67% 1RM | 67–85% 1RM | 85–100% 1RM |
| Rest | < 30 seconds | 30–90 seconds | 1.5–3 minutes |

## Rest Between Workouts

Endurance training can take place every day, but you wouldn't do the same workout every day, because of the risk of overuse injury. The same goes for strength training. You can strength train every day, but you have to do different workouts so that your muscles can recover. Because of the higher-intensity work that your muscles do during strength training, the rule is to let them rest 48 hours before working them again. If you want to add strength training into your daily schedule, you just have to split your workout so that some muscles get to rest while others are working. A common approach is to split your workouts into upper- and lower-body days or to split up the muscle

| TABLE 2.4 | Split program designs |
|---|---|

**2-day split**

Day 1: Chest, Triceps, Shoulders

Day 2: Legs, Biceps, Back

**3-day split**

Day 1: Legs, Shoulders

Day 2: Biceps, Back

Day 3: Chest, Triceps

groups so that you train complementary muscles together on different days (split program). Table 2.4 illustrates some common split program designs.

Complete rest occurs in 48 hours, but after 96 hours you actually get too much rest. How is that possible? If you rest too long, your body will decide that it doesn't need to maintain its new level of ability, so it will actually start to downgrade. This is the basic "use it or lose it" rule. Everything you do in training is designed to improve your body systems, but your body is inherently lazy and wants to maintain minimal homeostasis (the least amount of work it has to do). So after 96 hours without another workout stimulus to keep it going, your body starts to return to baseline.

To prevent this decline, establish a routine for strength training with no more than 2 days of rest between workouts. For example, if you want to use an entire-body workout, you need to do it at least every 3 days. If you split up your workout into smaller pieces, make sure that you work each muscle group again between 48 and 96 hours later. Chapter 7 explores some training programs that you can use as guidelines.

# 3

# Progression Systems:
# How to Keep Moving Forward

**N**o strength training program will be successful if there isn't a plan for changing it once the body has adapted. The same is true for endurance training. Rather than setting a goal and stopping once you've achieved it, you set a new goal. In strength training, the goals aren't as specific as increasing your swim splits by a certain amount of time or running a particular distance; they are about continuously improving rather than getting to a certain point. There are several different ways of progressing a strength training workout, and different systems will work for different people. No one system is inherently better than another. This chapter discusses some of the more commonly used systems for athletes, each of which has its advantages and strengths. You need to find one that works with your overall training program.

## PRINCIPLE OF OVERLOAD

Progression is about effecting change in a program. When considering how to make a strength training program more difficult, often the first thing that comes to mind is increasing the weight, but in fact overload comes in many forms. The principle of overload states that for adaptation to occur, the body must be subjected to a stimulus that is greater than what it is used to. This stimulus can be in the form of more weight (intensity), reps, or sets; additional exercises; or less rest between sets. As long as what you choose makes the workout a little harder, that's overload.

Without overload, all you have is maintenance. Because you are seeking to do more than maintain your fitness, overload has to happen. As soon as you have adapted to a new overload, it is time to add another one. The progression systems in this chapter outline specific ways to know when adaptation has taken place and it is time for a new stimulus.

When deciding which component to change to produce overload, look at how each small change affects the entire workout. Exercise volume, mentioned in the discussion of sets and reps in Chapter 2, is affected by each of the other components. To begin with, volume is a calculation that basically tells you how much total weight you lifted during a workout. The equation is Sets $\times$ Reps $\times$ Weight. Rest time is not part of the calculation because it is the only variable that makes a workout more difficult when it is reduced rather than increased. If you leave everything else in the equation as is and reduce the amount of rest between sets, that creates an overload, even though exercise volume hasn't changed. In addition, you must calculate volume for each exercise and add the volumes together to get a total for each workout. If you are using the same sets, reps, and weight for several exercises, you can modify the calculation to Sets $\times$ Reps $\times$ Weight $\times$ Number of Exercises.

The smallest change you can make to volume is to increase repetitions by 1. Although that tiny change is an overload because it's more than you are used to, it is not a significant one. On the other hand, adding another set increases volume significantly because you are adding several repetitions. Adding another exercise changes volume even more because you are adding several new sets. The effect of changing the weight you use depends on how much weight is added.

## PRINCIPLE OF OVERLOAD

This principle states that the body will only adapt, improve, and change when it is subjected to a stimulus that is greater than what it is used to. A lack of overload results in maintenance only, or even loss of fitness.

One of the best ways to determine whether your workout is successful is to track your exercise volume over time. Keeping track of exercise volume is simple, but you have to pay attention to all the numbers and not mix them up. Remember, if you are using different weights on several different exercises, you have to calculate the volume for each of those exercises individually and add them all together at the end.

## THE 2-FOR-2 RULE

The simplest form of progression that an athlete can use is linear progression, based on the 2-for-2 Rule, which states that when you can complete 2 additional repetitions on the last set of an exercise for 2 consecutive workouts, it is time to progress by adding a new overload. This new overload can be in the form of more reps, another set, less rest between sets, or more weight. The 2-for-2 Rule requires you to use a set number of reps and sets for each workout (3 sets of 15, for example). It also requires you to push yourself on the last set, when you are the most fatigued.

The 2-for-2 Rule takes into account that most people have good and bad days, when their ability to work out is improved or hampered by outside forces (nutrition, sleep, emotions, stress, etc.). On those days when everything falls into place and you are having a great workout, those extra 2 reps may be easy, but on days when you are struggling to even get through the workout, those extra 2 reps may be completely out of the question. The 2-for-2 Rule prevents premature overload by making sure that the first time you achieved an extra 2 reps on the last set wasn't just a fluke. By doing 2 consecutive workout performances with the extra 2 reps, you can be sure that you are actually ready to move forward. This is a simple way to gauge readiness to overload or change the workout. The next workout should have a new overload to challenge your new capability.

The 2-for-2 Rule progression strategy is great for athletes who like a simple workout plan without a lot of complicated numbers. Having a specific number of sets and reps for each workout makes everything simple. It also requires you to be able to push yourself when you are the most tired, which is especially challenging at the end of a workout.

## CIRCULAR PROGRESSION

Circular progression is a little more complicated than the 2-for-2 Rule because you will work within the ranges of repetitions for each goal, rather than using a set number of reps for each set (refer to Table 2.3 for these ranges). In circular progression you start by establishing your goal for each exercise. For example, if you are training for hypertrophy, you will use 6 to 12 reps for each set. Instead of trying to finish a certain number within the range, you will always strive to reach the highest number of reps for that goal (in this case 12). So during every set, your goal is to get 12 reps. When you achieve 12 reps, it's time to progress by inserting a new overload. The most common, and easiest, component to change in circular progression is the weight.

Because of the inverse relationship between repetitions and weight, if you add more weight to produce overload, you will complete fewer reps. This is exactly what you want to happen. If you make just a small increase in weight, your repetitions should still be within the range for your goal. For example, increasing weight reduces your reps to 8 on the next set. Now you have to keep working with that weight until you can complete a set of 12. Then it's time to increase the weight again. As its name implies, this system keeps going around: increasing reps, then weight, then reps again, then weight again (see Figure 3.1).

An important point to remember when using circular progression is that for it to work correctly, you have to put forth your best effort on every set, especially the first. You should always complete the most reps on your first set, because you are the least fatigued when you start that set. If you do more reps on the second, third, or fourth set of an exercise, then you really weren't giving it your all at the beginning. When you do reach the maximum number of repetitions for your goal, the new overload must occur on the very next set. This differs from the 2-for-2 Rule, which allows for some variation in effort. Circular

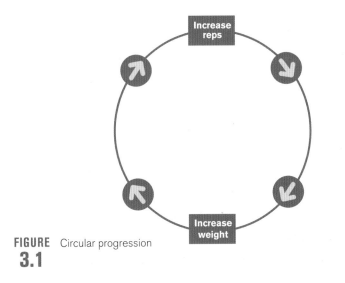

**FIGURE**  Circular progression
**3.1**

progression assumes that if you can do it once, you can do it again, so there is no waiting to make the overload adjustment.

The benefit of circular progression is that it makes ongoing adjustments based on your performance. You are not tied to a set number of repetitions but are allowed to push yourself constantly. In addition, because of the relationship between reps and weight, as long as you are training within the correct range of repetitions, you will also be using the correct percent 1RM for your goal. You do not have to retest after you have made improvements; the exercise adjusts automatically with you. This style of progression requires a healthy amount of motivation from you, but if you give it your all, you will see improvements on a regular basis.

## PERIODIZATION

Since the early 1990s, periodization of training programs has grown in popularity, starting with professional and Olympic athletes and working its way out to the general public. If planned and used correctly, periodization can offer some benefits that the 2-for-2 Rule and circular progression alone cannot. Periodization is so effective because it is built on the concept of sequenced potentiation, which is a method of building on previous goals or ability. For instance, you could train for more strength, or you could train first for hypertrophy, and then train for strength. The latter sequence takes the increased muscle size and builds strength from that, whereas the former just builds strength from the muscle you already have. If the goal is increased strength, periodization allows you to build up to a higher level of strength than a regular training program does.

Periodized programs are built one period at a time. The periods of training are grouped together to serve one overall goal, which could be muscular endurance, hypertrophy, strength, or power. Each period is called a *cycle*. The overall program is called the *macrocycle*, which has the overall goal. Within the macrocycle are two or more *mesocycles*, which divide the overall goal into smaller goals. Each of these smaller goals has a different physiological outcome, and each successive mesocycle builds on the results of the previous mesocycle. Finally, each

mesocycle is divided into two or more *microcycles*, in which the actual component programming is done. Each microcycle builds on the previous microcycle, until the goal of the mesocycle is reached. Figure 3.2 is a visual layout of a 3-month periodization program with 1-month mesocycles, each with 2-week microcycles.

Periodization can be adapted to just about any length of time. You can use it between triathlons or to train for one big one down the road. There are no rules about how long the macrocycle has to

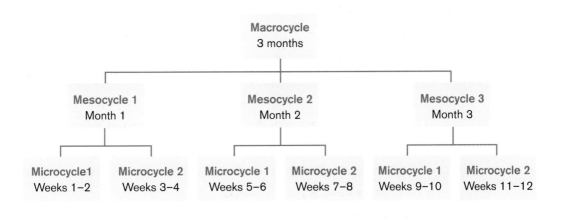

**FIGURE 3.2** Periodization cycles

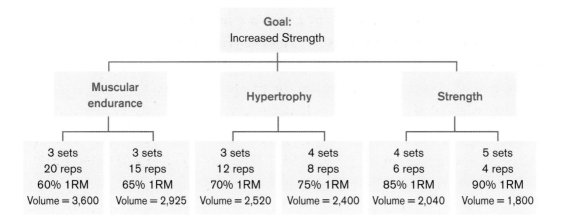

**FIGURE 3.3** Sample periodization program

be, as long as you can fit at least two mesocycles within one macrocycle, and at least two microcycles within each mesocycle. A good rule of thumb is to keep microcycles at least 1 to 2 weeks long so that your body can have time to adapt toward one goal before you move on to the next.

Choosing the macrocycle and mesocycle lengths is simple. The real work is putting together your microcycles, because this is where the real progression takes place. The idea is to have each microcycle build on the next, with an overall scheme of increasing intensity and decreasing volume over the course of each mesocycle and macrocycle. For example, using Figure 3.2 as a starting point, Figure 3.3 fills in the goals and components. The first mesocycle has a goal of muscular endurance, the second hypertrophy, and the third strength. Within each mesocycle, the microcycles include each of the required sets, reps, and percent 1RM that correlates with the mesocycle goal, and each microcycle increases in intensity and decreases in volume. Putting these numbers together is more an art than a science. As long as you stay within the ranges for each goal, and as long as the intensity rises and the volume decreases from microcycle to micro-cycle, you can't go wrong. There are numerous ways to use these guidelines to reach the same goal, which is another good thing about periodization. You can change the numbers to fit your training needs, time schedule, and goals and always make improvements.

You can change the numbers to fit your training needs, time schedule, and goals and always make improvements.

So far you have covered only the program components of sets, reps, and weight for your periodization program. You also have to include the actual exercises you want to use. Again, there are no rules about which exercises to use or when to change them. In fact, you can use entirely different exercises for each microcycle—yet another way of introducing overload in this progression. When calculating your volume, the easiest way to incorporate the number of exercises you are using is to keep the number the same, for example always using 10 exercises. But you can also start the program with basic exercises that you are good at and progress to more difficult exercises. This makes your body not only work harder as the program moves along, but learn new skills as well.

## TAPERING STRENGTH TRAINING

As in any type of training program, in the days leading up to a competition you should reduce the amount and intensity of training to allow your body to fully recuperate prior to the event. With strength training, you should maintain intensity while decreasing frequency, then volume. Typically, tapering strength training 7 to 10 days before an event, with at least 3 full days of rest before the event, is suggested.

Begin by decreasing the frequency of your training sessions, allowing more rest days between each one. If you are using a split program, switch to a full-body training program so that you can decrease the number of training days and not leave any muscle groups untrained. You may need to decrease the number of exercises you are using for each muscle group, so focus on those exercises that you feel will benefit you most.

Next, decrease exercise volume to a low level, but maintain the same intensity (amount of weight). Research has shown that you can maintain fitness levels for a short period of time if the intensity of training is maintained while the frequency and volume of training are decreased. This effect lasts only a short time before the body begins to lose fitness, so don't start tapering too early.

# PART II

# Program Preparation

# 4

# Strength Training
# Tools and Equipment

**I**n any health club, gym, or fitness center you will find a wide array of choices in exercise equipment. There are more than 50 manufacturers of gym equipment. In addition, late-night television commercials offer exercise techniques and special equipment that are supposed to provide results that no other products can. With all these choices, how do you know what equipment is useful, and what just doesn't work?

When you're trying to build a strength training program that is specific for triathlons, not every exercise or piece of equipment will be right for you, even if it does work the right muscle. The equipment has to provide the correct stimulus to the appropriate muscle in the right direction. Unfortunately, not much equipment has been designed with triathlons in mind. Most equipment is built with ease of use and eye appeal in mind, and much of it doesn't do what it was intended to.

This chapter provides a foundation you can use to determine whether a piece of equipment will suit your needs. Because more and newer designs are released every year, it is important that you be able to scrutinize equipment to get the best return for your money and effort.

## FREE WEIGHTS VERSUS MACHINES

There is a long-standing argument about whether free weights or exercise machines are better. Free weights have been around longer than machines. Ancient Greeks lifted different-sized rocks as exercise. There is a story about a man named Milo who supposedly lifted a bull calf every day of its life—effectively lifting more and more weight as the bull grew. In the early 1970s, Universal Equipment brought out a lineup of chrome-plated equipment that introduced exercise machines to the general public.

It doesn't really matter whether free weights or machines are "better." No one piece or type of equipment is better than another; they are just different. It's the differences that may make a particular style better in one instance, and less effective in another instance. What matters is exactly what you are trying to do and what equipment will provide that result.

A *free weight* is anything that provides resistance, is free to move in any direction, and is not attached to an immovable object or a base. Examples are weight plates, barbells, dumbbells, ankle weights, and even the body (dumbbells and barbells are abbreviated DB and BB in later chapters). A free weight doesn't have to be made of iron or steel, or even have a handle. A sack of groceries, your bike, and your luggage can all be free weights. A free weight can be just about anything you can pick up and move.

A *machine* is a piece of equipment that moves in only one direction no matter how you push or pull on it. Machines are usually designed to do only one thing, such as knee extensions, so they cannot be used for other muscle groups, other joints, or any other motion. Machines are therefore relatively limited compared with free weights.

Within the machine category, there are two distinct styles: plate loaded and selectorized. Selectorized machines have a stack of plates for resistance. You choose the resistance by inserting a pin under the weight you want to use. Plate loaded machines require you to add free weight plates to the machine to increase resistance. They are sometimes marketed as a combination of free weight and machine equipment, but the only free weight component is picking up a plate and putting it on the machine, which is not part of the actual exercise.

A few factors really highlight the differences between machines and free weights. Machines provide a stable environment in which you have to concentrate only on moving the machine. They are safer than free weights because you can't drop them on your toes, they usually have a seat that provides support and extra leverage for pushing against, and they are easy to learn to use. Free weights require additional coordination and balance, which machines have built in. The extra work required to use free weights properly means that other muscles are being used to keep your posture and technique correct during the exercise. For example, if you use a biceps curl machine (Figure 4.1), the machine makes sure your arms are kept in the right place, you get to sit down so there is no upsetting your posture, and all you have to do is pull the weight up. On the other hand, using a free weight such as a barbell to

**FIGURE 4.1** Biceps curl machine. Note that the arm pad and seat properly position the body and keep anything but the arms from moving.

**FIGURE 4.2** Free weight barbell curl. The body must work to stand and perform the exercise with good technique because there are no pads to lean against.

do a biceps curl (Figure 4.2) requires you to use your legs and back muscles to maintain a standing posture, especially as the weight is brought up, and there is a tendency to lean back to balance it. You have to maintain the correct arm position as well because there is no pad to rest against. Machines therefore have the advantage of making the exercise more focused (you don't have to do anything but pull on the weight), which can make them safer for beginners. On the other hand, because free weight exercises require other muscles to provide support (your legs and back), they create a more realistic situation because your body is not supported at every angle. This is more difficult and requires more practice to maintain correct form.

Machines have the advantage of making the exercise more focused (you don't have to do anything but pull on the weight), which can make them safer for beginners.

Because a machine can do only one thing, sometimes there isn't one that works the movement you want to perform. However, you can accomplish just about every exercise imaginable with free weights if you use your imagination. Free weights don't take up much space and can be used for several exercises. With machines, on the other hand, you require a different one for every exercise in your program, so space becomes an issue quickly for those considering a home gym.

Is there a machine that is better suited for the movement you want to perform, or is a free weight the better option? Depending on the exercise, how specific the movement is, and the amount of resistance you need to apply, the answer can go either way. Again, one is not better; they are just different. A combination of free weight and machine exercises is used in later chapters, and each is chosen because of its practical application and benefits for the triathlete.

## USER-DEFINED CABLES

Another type of equipment referred to often in this book is cables, technically called "user-defined cables" because the user decides how the equipment is used. For example, a low pulley cable could be used for several different hip exercises, as well as for some upper-body exercises such as biceps curls. Cable equipment comes in several forms, from large, multistation pieces, to single low- or high-pulley pieces, to the newest styles that allow you to move the pulley anywhere from the floor to above your head with a simple adjustment (Figure 4.3).

User-defined cables are beneficial because they allow you to choose a movement that fits your body size and your particular movement patterns. A machine moves in only one direction, so you can't make adjustments to make it fit you. A cable moves where you tell it to, so it always fits your body. A free weight should do the same thing, but a free weight works only when you are lifting the weight up, whereas a cable can be set so that you are pushing the handles (and therefore the resistance) directly out in front of you, or even down toward the ground. Because gravity works in only one direction with free weights, that limits their use for some movements.

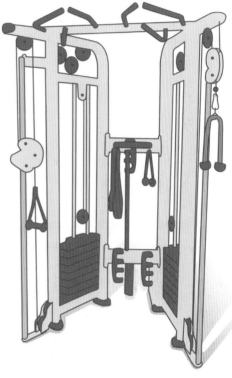

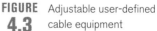

**FIGURE** Adjustable user-defined
**4.3** cable equipment

## BODY WEIGHT

Body weight as an important source of resistance during triathlon training has been discussed in Chapter 2. In fact, your body weight is the one type of resistance that you can't get rid of (unless you are training in outer space). Just the act of sitting up or standing is an exercise against gravity. When you are doing other strength training exercises, the weight of your body isn't usually figured into the amount of resistance, but it's always there. We don't count it because it is too difficult to measure. You can stand on a scale and see how much you weigh, but you never really lift your whole body weight except in exercises such as dips or chin-ups. When doing a leg extension, you lift the weight you have selected, plus the weight of your leg from the knee down. How much more is that? It is not practicable to weigh just part of your body, so we normally just accept that it's there and ignore it. This is fine, but be aware that it is part of the equation.

## RESISTANCE TUBING

Resistance tubing comes in several different forms. The most common and useful for your purposes is the style that has handles at both ends (Figure 4.4). Most tubing comes in lengths of about 4 feet, and there are several different thicknesses so that you can vary the resistance. Unlike free weights or machines, which have a fixed amount of resistance, tubing's resistance becomes greater the farther you stretch it. For example, a 10-pound dumbbell is always going to weigh 10 pounds, but a piece of tubing may start out relatively easy and become "heavier" as you stretch it.

Resistance tubing uses potential energy to provide more resistance the more you stretch it. *Potential energy* describes the amount of energy an object has stored up as a result of its position. If you hold a dumbbell in the air, it has potential energy. As soon as you let go of it, it will fall to the floor and

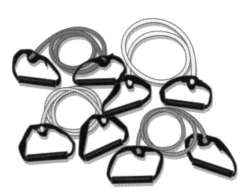

**FIGURE 4.4**   Variety of resistance tubing sizes

hit with a certain amount of force. Resistance tubing will break if you stretch it too far, but if it does, you can fix it by tying the two ends back together. The tubing will be a little shorter, but it will still work.

Choosing the correct tubing for a particular exercise involves trial and error. Start with a light piece of tubing and move up, to avoid injury. You can get several different sizes of tubing to give yourself a variety of resistances, or you can double up and use two pieces of the same-size tubing to double the resistance. When you make a piece of tubing shorter by choking up on the handles or wrapping it around a support pole a few times before starting your exercise, you effectively increase the resistance it will provide (but

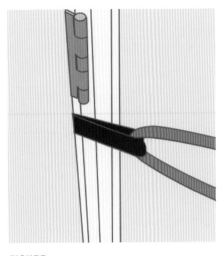

**FIGURE 4.5** Tubing anchor placed in doorway

also the chance that it will stretch too far and break, so be careful).

Most exercises using resistance tubing require the tubing to be attached to an anchor so you can pull or push on the handles. If you have a machine or pole, you can simply wrap the tubing around it at various heights according to the exercise instructions. If you are exercising at home, a tubing anchor that is inserted through the opening between a door and the doorframe is the perfect solution (Figure 4.5). When the door is shut, the anchor provides a solid place to loop your tubing through, and the door will not be damaged. Never just shut the door on your tubing, thinking that the door will hold it in place—the tubing will tear.

Because resistance tubing can be anchored in any position, it's similar to a cable. The difference is in the resistance: The cable provides constant resistance, whereas the tubing has progressive resistance. If you find an exercise that requires cable equipment but do not have access to such equipment, you can substitute resistance tubing and perform the exercise exactly the same way.

**FIGURE 4.6** Stability balls are sized according to height

## STABILITY BALLS

Stability balls, also called Swiss balls, are a great tool to introduce an unstable platform for exercise and provide a support during exercises in which a regular exercise bench just can't do the job. They can take the place of any type of exercise bench or seat for most free weight and resistance tubing exercises and are an important part of some core exercises.

Stability balls come in several sizes. The right size for you depends on your height (see Figure 4.6). When you sit on top of a stability ball, the tops of your thighs should be parallel to the floor. If your knees are higher than your hips, the ball is too short; if your knees are lower than your hips, the ball is too tall. Keep the ball properly inflated. It should flatten out somewhat when you sit or lie on it, but it should always be inflated enough so that it rolls around under you. A ball that is too flat increases the stability of the platform, which is the opposite of what you want.

## MEDICINE BALLS

Medicine balls are an old-fashioned free weight. They have been around for a long time but have recently resurfaced as a prime exercise tool, especially for core exercises. Some are hard and bounce like a basketball; some are soft and don't bounce at all (Figure 4.7). What matters is how much it weighs (between 10 and 15 pounds is best) and its

**FIGURE 4.7** Selection of medicine balls

size (which should be about the size of a basketball or volleyball). The medicine ball is heavy compared with most sport balls, but you won't be kicking or throwing it for any distance, and the weight of the ball is its greatest benefit. It provides resistance in an unusual form. Most weights we deal with come in the form of something with a handle, but a medicine ball requires both hands to control because it doesn't have a handle. Although it is a little ungainly and takes some practice, once you get the hang of it, it is quite fun and very effective.

## ANKLE WEIGHTS

**FIGURE 4.8** Adjustable ankle weights

Ankle weights are often overlooked as a source of resistance. By strapping an ankle weight around your leg just above your foot, you increase your body weight by that amount. You can get ankle weights that are adjustable (Figure 4.8), usually from 1 to 10 pounds, so you have some room to increase the resistance over time. Any exercise that involves lifting your legs off the floor, including lunges, step-ups, and leg lifts, can be made a little more challenging with an ankle weight.

# 5

# Warm-Up, Cool-Down, and Flexibility

**P**roper **warm-up, cool-down,** and flexibility add to the effectiveness of training by preparing your body for work, helping your body recover from the workout, and making sure you can move through the proper range of motion. Quite often the warm-up, cool-down, and flexibility portions of a workout are minimized or completely ignored. This would be like training for the swim and bike, but never running. A training program is complete only if every component is sufficiently included. There are many physiological benefits to warming up before exercise, some life-saving reasons to cool down after a workout, and lots of stress reduction to be found in a flexibility program. This chapter details some of the truths and myths about these training components and provides the information you need to put together a well-rounded program.

## GETTING YOUR BODY READY

As a dedicated triathlete, you wouldn't get out of bed in the morning, put on your running shoes, and immediately start jogging without warming up. If you have been around triathlons for any time, you have seen other athletes doing a few laps in the pool or lake, riding their bikes, or jogging around the transition area. They do this to better prepare their bodies for the challenges ahead. Warming up has long been part of an endurance athlete's preparations, and it is also a misunderstood part of strength training.

There are a number of claims about what a warm-up does to help prepare the body to lift weights: that it increases blood flow to the muscles, increases the muscle temperature, and alerts the central nervous system. While this is all true, that's not the end of the story. Warm-ups for cardio exercise and for resistance exercise are a little different. Typical cardio exercise is done for several minutes continuously, so the benefits listed above do occur. However, a traditional strength training warm-up is usually done by completing one or two sets of an exercise with a really light weight before completing the assigned sets and reps with a normal weight. These extra sets take only a few seconds each, with some rest in between and then more rest before starting the real workout. As a result of these rest periods, the increase in blood flow and muscle temperature that you want isn't retained. The body responds to exercise by increasing blood flow to the working muscles, but when work stops, blood flow to those muscles is reduced very quickly. Likewise, it takes continuous work—in the range of 10 minutes—to increase muscle temperature, so doing a couple of short sets does not help. Although it is true that the central nervous system is alerted because any movement that simulates the work about to be done allows the brain to start sending the correct motor pattern signals to the muscles, for this to work with strength training, you would need to do a warm-up before each exercise rather than just a single warm-up prior to your workout.

Traditional warm-up sets are not what you need to effectively prepare for strength training, but a short warm-up on a cardio machine that uses both the upper and lower body is. Examples are light jogging on a treadmill without holding on (your arms have to work), using a rowing machine, and using an elliptical machine or bike that has moving arm handles. Any of these will get blood flowing to all your limb muscles, and if you do the work for about 10 to 15 minutes, your muscle temperature will increase as well. A higher muscle temperature allows the energy processes to work faster, leads to faster removal of by-products such as lactate, and creates quicker muscle contractions.

If you still want to do a light warm-up set before your heavier lifting, you need to go directly to the exercise, do a light warm-up, and then immediately start your regular routine. After you start your workout, your body may cool back down between sets, but not very much. Your heart rate won't return to resting, so you will be pumping blood to the muscles much more quickly as long as you are working out. The short rests between sets will cause a small reduction in blood flow and temperature, but the initial elevation will help carry you through your workout. The key is to limit your rest time between sets as much as possible. This is where grouping your exercises so that you can work one area while another is resting helps maintain blood flow and temperature. Even walking around in between sets is better than sitting and waiting for the next set. As long as you keep moving, your body will stay warmed up and ready to exercise.

## WORKOUT RECOVERY

Your body does not go right back to its resting level immediately after cessation of exercise. Heart rate and ventilation remain at a higher level for a short time while your body continues to remove metabolic by-products from muscle, replenish energy stores, and reduce body heat. As part of your cardio training, you may exercise at a low level to help your cool-down, or you may take a short walk until your heart rate returns to resting and you have stopped sweating. In strength training, you need to aim for the same objectives.

Probably the most important reason to cool down is to prevent blood pooling in the legs. During exercise, the heart pumps blood down to the legs (with the help of gravity), and the contractions of leg muscles push blood back to the heart to be recirculated. The heart is a great pump, but it's only good at pushing blood out, not sucking it back in—that requires a "muscle pump," which works only if you are moving. If you stop moving, the extra blood that was sent to the muscles during exercise doesn't make its way back to the heart fast enough, and the heart has to work harder—keeping the heart rate higher for longer. In extreme circumstances, such as very hard training, exercising in the heat, or training only the lower-body muscles, this pooling can reduce the blood return to the heart so much that it puts excessive strain on the heart.

You should start your cool-down immediately after your last set and continue for as long as it takes to get your heart rate and breathing back to near resting.

Cooling down can be simply walking around until your heart rate returns to near resting, or doing just about any light cardio exercise. You should start your cool-down immediately after your last set and continue for as long as it takes to get your heart rate and breathing back to near resting. How long this takes will vary with the intensity of your workout (it takes longer to cool down from a hard workout). The cool-down can be lower-body exercise only, because gravity takes care of returning the upper-body blood back to the heart. Stretching and flexibility training are not considered a cool-down—especially static stretching. Movement makes the "muscle pump" work, and static stretching isn't moving, so it is not an effective cool-down.

## STRETCHING TO MOVE

Stretching has long been touted as an important component of any fitness program, but it is especially important in strength training. Stretching before and after your cardio training to keep your muscles from getting tight is only part of the benefit. *Flexibility* is the ability to move the body in a wide range of purposeful movements at a required speed. It determines how we move. If your body is not capable of moving through the range of motion that is required for an exercise, you can't do that exercise properly. If an exercise movement is difficult and makes you feel like you are being stretched, that is because you don't have the flexibility you need to move through the required range of motion. The exercise movement should never be difficult to do or seem like a stretch by itself.

During strength training you should always be able to complete an entire movement with ease—meaning you don't have to force your body into a particular position or through a particular movement. If you are not flexible enough, you will compensate by allowing another body part to relax and move, thus losing correct technique. For example, if during a squat your heels come up off the floor, it's because your calf muscles are too tight. As a result, you alter the exercise technique by lifting your heels so you can continue to squat down to the required position. Instead of doing the exercise right, you position yourself for injury. The solution is to improve your flexibility. An exercise is dangerous only when it's done wrong, and not being flexible enough to maintain correct technique is just plain dangerous. The benefit of a proper stretching program is that it will allow you to move through the required range of motion for any exercise and help prevent injury.

Stretching does not reduce soreness. That idea has been around for a long time, but there is no research to support it. Soreness is mainly the result of eccentric muscle actions and is a signal that some small amount of damage has been done. You will remain sore until the damage is repaired. Fortunately, soreness is usually temporary. No amount of stretching will make you less sore. It may make you less tight, which makes it easier to move, but it will not repair injury.

Likewise, stretching does not prevent injuries from occurring at all, especially during competition. Proper flexibility will prevent injury due to improper technique by allowing you to move as you should, but it will not prevent other injuries. Research has shown that the quantity and variety of injuries suffered by athletes in many different sports are the same whether they stretch or not.

A proper flexibility training program should be approached with just as much dedication as your cardio or strength training. If you make time to swim, bike, run, or lift weights, you must make time to stretch. I have often seen people spend 30 to 45 minutes in the gym lifting weights and less than 5 minutes stretching, which is just not enough. Flexibility training should be completed every time you strength train and should include every muscle you have trained.

To increase and retain flexibility, each static stretch, such as those described in this chapter, must be held from 30 to 60 seconds. If you are stretching each of your major muscle groups (biceps, triceps, shoulders, upper and lower back, chest, abdominals, hips, thighs, hamstrings, and calves), you will spend approximately 20 to 30 minutes in a minimal flexibility program.

Flexibility is something that everyone can improve upon, even if that improvement comes slowly. Stretching should follow the same rules as progression for strength training: If you progressively stretch a little farther than you did before, you will increase your flexibility over time. Some muscles respond quickly and show great improvement, while others seem to barely move. But you won't see any improvement if you don't stretch, so no matter how little benefit you see, keep going—it will happen.

A general rule for how far to stretch is to do so into the uncomfortable zone, but not to the point of pain. You should feel a stretch, but it shouldn't hurt. The uncomfortable feeling of a stretch should go away as soon as you stop stretching; if it doesn't, then you went too far. It is better to let your body adjust slowly rather than to push hard just to try to get that extra little bit. Muscles will tear during a stretch, so you have to be careful, listen to your body, and know your limitations. Injuries during stretching are rare, but they do happen.

The remainder of this chapter illustrates stretches that cover all the major muscle groups. Each stretch includes directions and how long you should do it. You can choose which stretches to do depending on what areas you work during each training session. There are far too many stretches possible to include them all here, and there may be others you want to add to your program. That's fine, as long as you follow the guidelines for safety and duration outlined above.

## BICEPS TWISTERS

Hold both arms straight out in front of you, hands open and fingers together. Now rotate your palms down and keep rotating them until they face out to the sides and you feel the stretch through your biceps (Figure 5.1). You won't feel obvious stretch on this one because the biceps don't have many nerve endings. Hold the stretch for a full 60 seconds, constantly trying to rotate a little more.

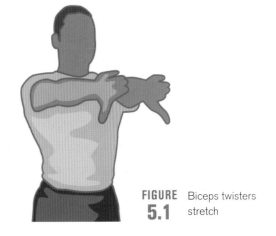

**FIGURE 5.1** Biceps twisters stretch

## TRICEPS PRETZEL

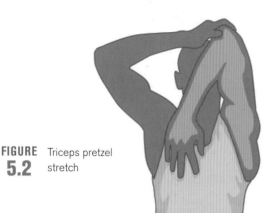

**FIGURE 5.2** Triceps pretzel stretch

Reach up and over your head with one hand and then reach as far down your back as you can. Pull on that elbow with the other hand to get a little farther down (Figure 5.2); feel the stretch in your triceps. Hold for 30 seconds, then stretch the other arm.

## SHOULDER CROSS-PULL

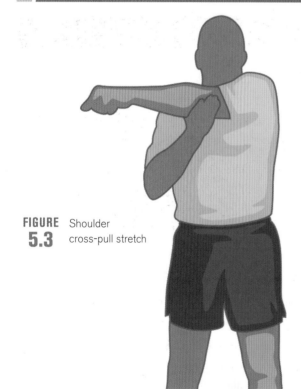

**FIGURE 5.3** Shoulder cross-pull stretch

Reach across your chest with one arm and hold that arm's elbow with your other hand. Keep your arm just under your chin and as straight as possible (Figure 5.3). Using the hand on your elbow, push the arm against your chest until you feel the stretch across the back of your shoulder. If you don't feel much tension, raise your arm a little higher under your chin. Hold for 30 seconds, then stretch the other shoulder.

## SHOULDER TURNAROUND

Stand so you are facing a wall. Place the palm of one hand against the wall at shoulder height. Now turn your body away from the wall, but keep your palm flat against it (Figure 5.4). If your right hand is on the wall, turn to your left, and vice versa. Keep turning your body until you feel the stretch in your shoulder, then hold that position for 30 seconds. Relax, then repeat for the other shoulder.

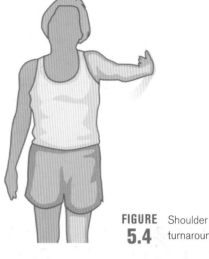

**FIGURE 5.4** Shoulder turnaround stretch

## CHEST BOW

**FIGURE 5.5** Chest bow stretch

Kneel on the floor in front of a chair, exercise bench, or stability ball. Place both hands on top of the object and scoot back until you are reaching forward to keep your hands on it. Drop your head between your arms and push your shoulders toward the floor, trying to make a straight line from your hands to your hips (Figure 5.5). Hold this position for 60 seconds, then relax.

## ABDOMINAL ARCH

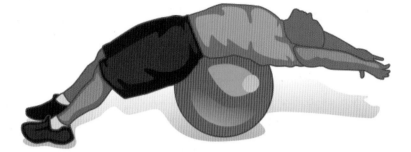

**FIGURE 5.6** Abdominal arch stretch

Lie on top of your stability ball face up, with the ball in the middle of your lower back. Stretch your legs out straight and point your toes toward the floor. Clasp your hands together and reach over your head as far as you can (Figure 5.6). Now let your back muscles relax while you try to touch your hands to the floor; this will stretch your abdominals. Keep breathing normally while you hold this position for 60 seconds.

## LOWER-BACK LEANING TOWER

Stand with your feet together and your knees slightly bent. Bend forward and hug your legs just above your knees. Allow your head and neck to relax while you use your arms to pull your chest as close to your thighs as possible (Figure 5.7). Keep breathing normally while you hold this position for 60 seconds.

**FIGURE 5.7** Lower-back leaning tower stretch

## UPPER-BACK POLE-PULL

Stand facing a pole, doorway opening, or exercise machine—anything tall and strong enough that it won't move when you pull on it. Grab the object at about waist height (if you are using a door, hold on to the door-knobs on each side) and step back about 2 feet. Keep your feet together and let your hips move back so your upper body leans forward (Figure 5.8). Now pull back on the pole, allowing your body weight to stretch your shoulders. Hold this stretch for 60 seconds.

**FIGURE 5.8** Upper-back pole-pull stretch

## HIP DIAGONALS

**FIGURE 5.9** Hip diagonals stretch right leg

**FIGURE 5.10** Hip diagonals stretch left leg

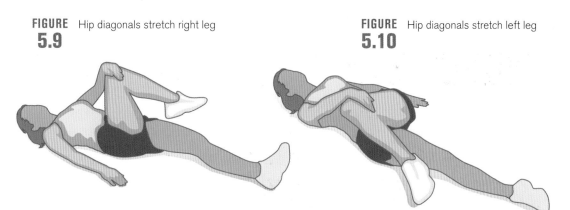

Lie on your back with your legs straight out on the floor and your feet together. Bring your right knee up toward your chest and grab hold of that knee with your left hand. Totally relax your leg and let your hand hold it in place. Your knee should be relaxed and your foot should be hanging down. Keeping your shoulders and hips on the floor, pull your knee across your body toward your left shoulder (Figure 5.9). If you aren't feeling the stretch in your hip, you probably aren't fully relaxed. Hold the stretch for 30 seconds, then repeat for the other side by pulling the left leg across your body with your right hand (Figure 5.10).

## HIP SIDE SKATE

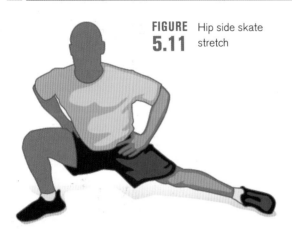

**FIGURE 5.11** Hip side skate stretch

Stand with your feet together and hands on your hips. Take a big step out to one side. The leg that stays in place should stay straight while the other leg bends. Bend down until you feel the stretch on the inside of the thigh of the straight leg (Figure 5.11). Hold for 30 seconds, then do the other side.

## QUAD STEP

**FIGURE 5.12** Quad step stretch

Facing away from a chair or exercise bench, bend one leg and place the toes of that foot on the edge of the object. You can use your stability ball, but it has to be still and not roll around. You can hold on to something for balance if you need to. With the other foot, take a big step forward. Try to keep your torso as upright as possible while pushing your hips toward the floor (Figure 5.12). Your back knee may touch the floor, but don't rest on it. If you don't feel the stretch in your quads, take a bigger step out. Hold the stretch for 30 seconds, then switch to the other side.

## HAMSTRING TOWEL-PULL

Lie on your back and bend your knees until your feet are about a foot from your buttocks. Point one leg straight up in the air and wrap a towel around it, either just below the knee or over the top of the ankle (the ankle position is preferred). Hold on to the ends of the towel with both hands and slowly pull the towel toward you so that your leg moves higher in the air (Figure 5.13). Pull until you feel the stretch in your hamstrings, then hold that position for 30 seconds. Now switch and stretch the other side.

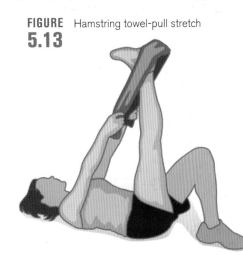

**FIGURE 5.13** Hamstring towel-pull stretch

## CALF WALL-STEP

Stand facing a wall or doorway. While keeping its heel on the floor, place the toes of one foot against the wall as high as you can. Your other foot should be behind you. Keep your body upright as you push your hips forward, and lean toward the wall until you feel the stretch in your front foot (Figure 5.14). If you don't feel the stretch, move your toes farther up the wall and really plant your heel on the floor so it doesn't move as you lean forward. Hold the stretch for 30 seconds, then repeat on the other side.

**FIGURE 5.14** Calf wall-step stretch

| TABLE 7.5 | Olympic-distance circuit 2: Training the same muscles on consecutive days |
| --- | --- |

**Emphasis:** Swimming–hypertrophy

**Order:** Push-pull

**4 sets of 10 reps with 70% 1RM:** Complete 1 set of each exercise in each circuit, then repeat until all sets are complete.

| Day 1: | Day 2: |
| --- | --- |
| DB shoulder press | Tubing stroke |
| Tubing kickback | Triceps push-down |
| Leg extension | Seated calf raise |
| Standing calf raise | Cable hip extension |
| One-arm throw | DB curl |
| Slam dunk | Bridging pullover |
| Cable lateral lift | Cable lateral cross |
| Inclined Superman | Lying leg curl |

is more advanced and should be used only after considerable training experience.

## Olympic Periodization

Periodized strength training programs for Olympic-distance triathlons take a little more time to plan because they are approximately twice as long as sprint-distance plans. This is quite good for the athlete who likes to spend more time adapting to a particular intensity of training before changing it up. In addition, the increase in percent 1RM from one microcycle to the next is smaller, so increases in weight are not as great a shock to the body. Finally, more mesocycles can be included, so more physiological goals can be focused on, although you do have the option of using only 2 mesocycles and goals if you like. Table 7.6

# 6

# Choosing Your
# Exercises and Order

Now that you understand the components of a total strength training program (including the warm-up, the cool-down, and flexibility), you can design a workout for your needs. This chapter leads you through choosing exercises that are best for you and arranging them in a workout. You can try several different approaches; one of the best things about strength training is that there are very few "carved in stone" rules. Using more than one program design will probably give you the results you need. A lot of trial and a little error will provide you with the best results.

## WHICH EXERCISES FIT YOU BEST

There are literally hundreds of different exercises, not all of them right for a triathlete. Chapters 8 through 14 contain the best exercises for triathletes because they focus on the movements and positions involved in training and competition. Even within this grouping there are still many exercises to choose from, and completing all of them in a single training session just isn't possible. Evaluating your personal strengths and weaknesses during and after training will lead you to the best exercises to improve your performance. Table 6.1 presents a strength training needs analysis to help you discover the areas you should concentrate on during strength training. Review the common symptoms in the analysis and use the solutions to guide you to the specific exercises you should incorporate into your training.

To figure out your areas of weakness, look at each portion of your triathlon training individually (swim, bike, and run), then in pairs (swim-bike and bike-run), then as a complete set. Analyzing your fatigue, aches and pains, or weakness during and after each event will help you understand which muscles need more work, which will then point you in the direction of the best exercises to include in your program. For each individual event, ask yourself which muscle groups feel the most fatigued or feel weaker than the others, or if a particular area of your body or muscle group becomes noticeably sore during or immediately after training or remains sore for longer than others. Focus your strength training on these groups.

Analyzing your fatigue, aches and pains, or weakness during and after each event will help you understand which muscles need more work.

When you complete endurance training in bricks or pairs (swim-bike or bike-run), analyze how each muscle group feels during the second event, after it has already been worked during the first event. For example, how do your legs feel during the bike after your swim, compared with how they feel during the bike when you don't swim first? If there is a big difference, you may need to spend more time training your legs to be stronger during the swim so they won't be so fatigued during the ride. Or if your upper body is significantly

working more on

pleting a triathlon,
and which are the
common mistake
fatigued because
If your shoulders
work.
rain every muscle
t is very important.
ng and your weak
be an imbalance.
knesses and bring
dy. Then you can

ur training (swim,
his case, focus on
this is to evaluate
instance, you may
the bike that you
omes time to run,

that is the most difficult. This indicates that you need to focus your strength training initially on improving your ability to swim and bike, so that you aren't so fatigued when they are done. Then you will have more left for the run.

There are many ways to choose which groups of exercises you need to do, and your focus will change as you make improvements, so reevaluation is essential. However, don't constantly change your program in an effort to find the right exercises. You have to let your body adapt before altering the program again. A good rule of thumb is to give yourself 6 to 8 weeks before rearranging your

| TABLE 6.1 | Weight training needs analysis |
|-----------|-------------------------------|

## Symptom

### Swimming

You have to rest your legs periodically and rely more on your arms.

You have to kick harder at times to let your arms rest.

Your body roll decreases the farther or longer you swim.

One leg becomes more tired than the other.

One arm or shoulder becomes more tired than the other.

You sometimes have to increase your stroke rate to maintain the same speed.

### Cycling

You push harder with one leg or the other.

Your thighs start to become tired before your hips and glutes do.

Your heels start to drop below your toes as you push on the pedals.

Your arms or shoulders become fatigued if you don't use aerobars.

Your shoulders or upper back become fatigued while using aerobars.

Your back sags instead of staying flat.

### Running

You drag your toes.

Your hamstrings become tired before your quads do.

Your quads become tired before your hamstrings do.

Your arms drop lower during long runs.

Your shoulders become tight or start to hurt.

You find yourself leaning forward.

Your strides become shorter as you run longer.

**Note:** *Refer to Appendix A for a list of exercises that will accomplish the solutions for each symptom.*

| Cause | Solution |
|---|---|
| relatively weak lower body | Strengthen quads, glutes, and hips. |
| relatively weak upper body | Strengthen shoulders, arms, and back. |
| core muscle fatigue | Add core exercises that work on rotation. |
| muscular imbalance in legs | Incorporate more single-leg exercises. |
| muscular imbalance in arms/shoulder | Incorporate more single-arm exercises. |
| not enough muscular endurance and weak upper body | Increase reps and number of upper-body exercises. |
| | |
| muscular imbalance in legs | Use more weight on single leg exercises for the weak side. |
| weak quadriceps | Incorporate more exercises that extend the knee. |
| weak calf muscles | Add more calf raises, step-ups, and walking lunges. |
| weak shoulders and/or arms | Train shoulders and triceps more. |
| weak shoulders and/or upper back | Strengthen the shoulders and upper back. |
| weak upper and lower back | Include more core exercises that strengthen the back. |
| | |
| weak shin muscles | Strengthen the dorsiflexor muscles. |
| muscle imbalance in thighs | Include more hamstring exercises. |
| muscle imbalance in thighs | Include more quad exercises. |
| biceps fatigue | Add more biceps exercises and repetitions. |
| bouncing and fatiguing shoulders | Focus more on shoulder strength for running. |
| lower back fatigue | Include more upright core exercises. |
| hip and glute fatigue | Increase exercises for hip and range of motion used. |

exercises, so that you can really tell whether your body is responding. Also remember that change is going to take place on the inside, so don't judge your results by what you see in the mirror. Listen to and feel your body as you train. If you are not as fatigued as before, everything is probably working fine, so don't try to change it right away. Find the exercises that stimulate your body to change positively and keep them in your program.

Give yourself 6 to 8 weeks before rearranging your exercises, so that you can really tell whether your body is responding.

You should enjoy the exercises you do. There is nothing worse than designing a program that you think will work, but that you hate doing. Odds are you won't put 100 percent effort into it, won't focus on the exercises, and will put off training as much as possible. There is a saying that the exercises you dislike the most are the ones you need the most. Although there is some truth to this, the other side of the coin is that you have to like training. A compromise may be to introduce exercises that you don't particularly care for one at a time. Give yourself an opportunity to get used to them and see how they make your body change. Don't load up on a lot of hard exercises that make you look for ways out of training. You can choose exercises just because you like them, but don't ignore what your body needs.

A word of caution: Any exercise that may cause a previous injury to flare up again should be avoided. For instance, if you have had an ACL injury, the leg extension exercise will place too much stress on your knee, so you should leave it out of your program. It is always a good idea to consult with a sports medicine physician if you are not sure whether an exercise could be problematic for you.

## HOW MANY EXERCISES FOR EACH BODY PART OR EVENT

The exercises in chapters 8 to 14 are divided into upper-body and lower-body exercises for each event (swim, bike, and run). The upper body includes anything above the waist, and the lower body is everything below the waist. After you have established what areas you need to concentrate on, decide how many exercises to have in your program. It is not a good idea to do every exercise in a section; that will definitely cause overtraining and decrease your performance. In a perfect world, you should be able to do 1 exercise for each muscle and get everything you need from it. However, our bodies are a little more complicated than that, because each muscle contributes and moves in several different ways depending on which event you are focusing on. For instance, all biceps exercises are not the same—and this applies to the exercises for any other muscle group.

A good rule to follow is never to do more than 3 exercises for any 1 muscle group during a single training session. You can choose 3 exercises from 1 event, or you can mix and match from 2 or 3 events, depending on what you need to accomplish. In addition, you should give a muscle time to recover after training, so never use the same exercises on 2 consecutive days. You can train the same muscle if you are not sore from the previous day's training, but use different exercises. This is an advanced way of training on consecutive days, which must be approached with caution and by paying very close attention to your body's responses and levels of fatigue and soreness.

## HOW MANY EXERCISES FOR EACH WORKOUT

To determine how many exercises you can finish in a single session, aim for 10 to 12 from a combination of different muscles and events. Part of this equation will be how much time you have to train. You can do more exercises in an hour than you can in 30 minutes. If time is a constraint, focus on the most important exercises first, and if there is time left over, move down your list to other exercises.

## EXERCISE ORDER

The order in which you complete your exercises will have a substantial impact on the effectiveness of each exercise and on the workout in general. There are several approaches to exercise order, each based on sound science, but none has been shown to be significantly better than another, so you can use each one to add variety to your workout.

### Goal-Oriented Order

The first exercise order places the emphasis on those areas that you feel need the most work. In this case, you will order each exercise in your workout according to how important it is to your total program. For example, if you feel that during the swim your shoulders are fatiguing too fast and are therefore a weak link, the exercises focusing on shoulder development for swimming should be the first ones you do. During a training session this allows you to work the areas of emphasis while you are fresh and full of energy. Later during the session, as you are getting tired, is not the time to try to work what you feel to be the most important area.

### Big Before Small

The next order arranges exercises according to the size of the muscle being worked. Larger muscles will require more energy, so they should be trained before fatigue sets in. For example, squats would come before leg extensions, followed by the seated toe raise. This ensures that the most fatiguing exercises are done first. Those exercises that involve relatively smaller muscle groups are saved for last because they require less energy production. This style of exercise order is based on the speed of metabolic energy depletion and restoration. During strength training, the main energy system is the ATP-PC (Adenosine triphosphate phosphogen) system, which supplies you with almost immediate energy to the muscles but lasts only about 10 seconds. When this is used up, the body relies on glycolysis to start converting stored glycogen to energy. This system lasts up to about 2 minutes. By that time you should have finished your set. Of key importance is not how fast these systems provide energy, but how fast they recover. It takes several minutes to recover the first ATP-PC system, so using it for the large muscle groups makes the most sense.

---

Those exercises that involve relatively smaller muscle groups are saved for last because they require less energy production.

---

## Hard to Easy

This exercise order is subjective, being based on psychology rather than physiology. If you start your workout with the most difficult exercises, rather than leaving them for last, you will be more likely to finish everything on your list. At one time or another, everyone has found a reason to skip out on the last part of a workout. Whatever the reason, skipping the hard exercise just makes it that much more difficult the next time. The less often you do an exercise, the slower your body will improve and adapt, which delays your performance progress. Doing a hard exercise first and getting it out of the way makes it much easier to complete the simple exercises.

## Multiple Joint to Single Joint

Arranging your exercises based on how many joints are involved is similar to arranging them based on muscle size. The more joints that are involved, the more muscle is involved. Not only that, but more joints moving during an exercise makes the exercise more complicated, so technique control is more difficult. It takes more focus and technique to do a tubing stroke exercise, which involves 3 joints, than to do a triceps push-down, which involves only 1 joint. Because proper technique is key to preventing injury and getting the most out of an exercise, it follows that those exercises that involve the most complicated maneuvers should be done first during a workout.

## Alternate Upper and Lower

Previous chapters discussed arranging exercises so that you could allow one body part to rest while another worked. One way of accomplishing this is by alternating upper-body and lower-body exercises. For the most part, these exercises are independent of each other. The only case in which they overlap is where the lower body supports the upper-body exercise while standing, which doesn't add much work to the lower body unless you just finished a difficult lower-body exercise and those muscles are fatigued. Switching between upper- and lower-body exercises keeps your heart pumping blood to different areas, so it gets an extra workout as well.

## Push-Pull

Another way of alternating exercises is by doing one push, then one pull, exercise. A push exercise is any action in which you are pushing a weight away from you (e.g., leg press, DB shoulder press, triceps push-down); a pull exercise brings the weight closer to you (e.g., biceps curl, lying leg curl, bridging pull-over). Not every exercise will clearly fall into a push or pull category (e.g., walking lunges, back extension, split squat), so this becomes a little fuzzy now and then. The basis for push-pull is that opposing muscle groups can be worked in order. For example, alternating a biceps curl with dips works both sides of the arms, so while the biceps are resting, the triceps work. Combining push-pull in an organization of opposing muscle groups is the most effective way to work this exercise order.

# 7

# Sample Training Programs

**I want to reiterate that there is no** single strength training program that will fit everyone. Likewise, every possible strength training program cannot be included in this chapter. It's up to you to put together the perfect plan for your needs and goals. This chapter provides an idea of the types of programs you can design, given the length of the triathlon you are training for and different exercise orders. These sample programs are based on the practices of athletes I have trained in the past, but that doesn't mean you should use them exactly as they are presented here. I cannot guarantee they will work for you because they were not designed for you. Look at how they are put together and substitute exercises you have chosen and workloads that are appropriate for your body to develop a program that will take you to new levels of performance.

## SPRINT DISTANCE

Sprint triathlons are more about speed than about endurance. You need cardiovascular endurance, but because the distances are shorter, you don't have to pace yourself for so long, and you can compete at a higher intensity. With higher cardiovascular intensity comes the need for more muscular power (the ability of muscles to contract very fast). In addition, because sprint triathlons are the shortest, you may be more likely to compete in a greater number of competitions per season, so you will need a strength training program that takes that into account. Following are a few possible workout designs that are very effective for sprint distances.

## Sprint Circuits

A circuit design program will have very short intervals between each exercise, basically only as long as it takes to get to the next exercise, and a repeating order of exercises. Instead of repeating sets of an exercise before moving on to the next one, you will complete 1 set of each exercise in your workout, then repeat that circuit until you have finished all your sets. It's up to you to decide the order of your exercises, but using alternating muscle groups is the most practical choice. A circuit program of 10 to 12 exercises will take only about 30 minutes. You can design several different circuits so that you have a different workout every day, or use the same one each time, as long as you allow enough rest time so your muscles are fully recovered from the last workout. Table 7.1 shows a circuit workout for a sprint-distance triathlete.

## Sprint Periodization

Because several sprint triathlons can be completed in a single season, a periodized plan for the sprint athlete will not require large amounts of time. The cycles will be short and the entire plan will be repeated between events. A 6-week periodization will provide enough time for 2

**TABLE 7.1**

| | Sprint-distance circuit program |
|---|---|

**Emphasis:** Cycling—muscular strength and power

**Order:** Multiple joint to single joint, alternating upper and lower body

**3 sets of 6 reps each with 85% 1RM:** Complete 1 set of each exercise in order, resting only long enough to move from one exercise to another. Repeat order until all 3 sets are complete.

**Exercises (and order):**

| | | | |
|---|---|---|---|
| 1. Step-up | 3. Glute press | 6. Back extension | 9. Single-leg extension |
| 2. DB (dumbbell) incline press | 4. Front raise | 7. Seated leg curl | 10. BB (barbell) wrist curl |
| | 5. Knee raise | 8. Shoulder dip | |

to 3 mesocycles to be completed, with microcycles lasting only 1 week. This means that you have to be prepared to change your intensity and volume every week, but not necessarily your exercises. You can opt to keep the same exercises for the entire macrocycle and change them only when you start a new macrocycle, or you can change exercises in each mesocycle. Table 7.2 shows a sample periodized program that contains 2 mesocycles with different exercises. Table 7.3 shows a sample periodized program with 3 mesocycles, with the same exercises but more changes in goal and intensity or volume.

## OLYMPIC DISTANCE

Olympic-distance triathletes need more endurance than sprint-distance triathletes, but there is still an emphasis on speed. Because of the longer distances, their muscles must be able to handle much more repetition and still provide the necessary force to keep them moving forward. Fewer Olympic-distance triathlons are typically completed in a season than sprint distances, so the amount of training between events

| TABLE 7.2 | Sprint-distance periodization program 1 |

**Emphasis:** Running—muscular endurance and hypertrophy

**Order:** Push-pull (upper- and lower-body pairs)

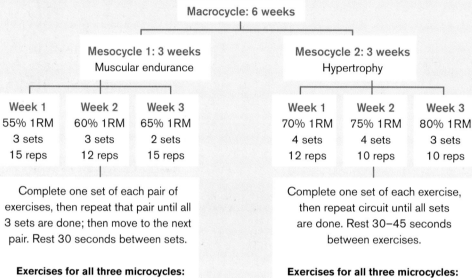

**Macrocycle: 6 weeks**

| Mesocycle 1: 3 weeks<br>Muscular endurance | Mesocycle 2: 3 weeks<br>Hypertrophy |
|---|---|

| Week 1<br>55% 1RM<br>3 sets<br>15 reps | Week 2<br>60% 1RM<br>3 sets<br>12 reps | Week 3<br>65% 1RM<br>2 sets<br>15 reps | Week 1<br>70% 1RM<br>4 sets<br>12 reps | Week 2<br>75% 1RM<br>4 sets<br>10 reps | Week 3<br>80% 1RM<br>3 sets<br>10 reps |

Complete one set of each pair of exercises, then repeat that pair until all 3 sets are done; then move to the next pair. Rest 30 seconds between sets.

Complete one set of each exercise, then repeat circuit until all sets are done. Rest 30–45 seconds between exercises.

**Exercises for all three microcycles:**

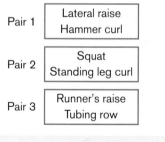

| Pair 1 | Lateral raise<br>Hammer curl |
|---|---|
| Pair 2 | Squat<br>Standing leg curl |
| Pair 3 | Runner's raise<br>Tubing row |

**Exercises for all three microcycles:**
Split squat
Single lying curl
Upright row
Shrugs
Leg press
Cable hip flex

is greater and takes place over a longer period of time. Periodized plans fit better with Olympic distances because more time can be spent in each microcycle, allowing the body to adapt more before moving on to the next microcycle or mesocycle. Circuit training also works and allows a triathlete to change his or her workout as often as desired with little planning.

TABLE
7.3
Sprint-distance periodization program 2

**Emphasis:** Swimming—muscular endurance, hypertrophy, and strength

**Order:** Big before small, double circuit (1 upper body, 1 lower body)

Macrocycle: 6 weeks

| Mesocycle 1: 2 weeks | | Mesocycle 2: 2 weeks | | Mesocycle 3: 2 weeks | |
|---|---|---|---|---|---|
| Muscular endurance | | Hypertrophy | | Strength | |
| Week 1 | Week 2 | Week 1 | Week 2 | Week 1 | Week 2 |
| 62% 1RM | 67% 1RM | 75% 1RM | 80% 1RM | 85% 1RM | 90% 1RM |
| 3 sets | 3 sets | 4 sets | 4 sets | 4 sets | 4 sets |
| 18 rep | 15 reps | 10 reps | 8 reps | 6 reps | 4 reps |

Complete one set of each exercise in a circuit, then repeat until all sets are done;
then do the same thing for the second circuit.

**Exercises for all microcycles:**

*Circuit 1 (lower body):*
Leg extension
Lying leg curl
Cable lateral lift
Seated calf raise

*Circuit 2 (upper body):*
Tubing stroke
DB shoulder press
Bridging pullover
One-arm throw
DB curl

## Olympic Circuits

Using circuit training combined with either circular progression
or the 2-for-2 Rule is very effective for Olympic-distance-triathlon
strength training. The use of more than 1 circuit allows more variety
and a greater training frequency (more days per week). Table 7.4
illustrates how you can use 2 circuits that train different body parts
on consecutive days. Table 7.5 shows how to train the same body
part on consecutive days with different exercises, although this

**Emphasis:** Cycling—muscular endurance; Running—strength

**Order:** Multiple joint to single joint

**Day 1:** Complete 1 set of each exercise in each circuit, then repeat until all sets are complete. (Note: You will complete the running lower-body circuit 1 more time than the cycling upper-body circuit.)

**Running lower-body circuit:** 4 sets of 6 reps with 87% 1RM

Leg press

Cable hip flex

Split squat

Seated toe raise

Standing leg curl

**Cycling upper-body circuit:** 3 sets of 15 reps with 65% 1RM

DB handle push-up

Shoulder dip

DB incline press

Front raise

**Day 2:** Complete 1 set of each exercise in each circuit, then repeat until all sets are complete.

**Cycling lower-body circuit:** 3 sets of 12 reps with 67% 1RM

Walking lunge

One-leg squat

Knee raise

Seated leg curl

Single-calf raise

**Running upper-body circuit:** 3 sets of 6 reps with 90% 1RM

Upright row

Tubing row

Lateral raise

Shrugs

**TABLE 7.5**

**Olympic-distance circuit 2: Training the same muscles on consecutive days**

**Emphasis:** Swimming–hypertrophy

**Order:** Push-pull

**4 sets of 10 reps with 70% 1RM:** Complete 1 set of each exercise in each circuit, then repeat until all sets are complete.

| Day 1: | Day 2: |
| --- | --- |
| DB shoulder press | Tubing stroke |
| Tubing kickback | Triceps push-down |
| Leg extension | Seated calf raise |
| Standing calf raise | Cable hip extension |
| One-arm throw | DB curl |
| Slam dunk | Bridging pullover |
| Cable lateral lift | Cable lateral cross |
| Inclined Superman | Lying leg curl |

is more advanced and should be used only after considerable training experience.

## Olympic Periodization

Periodized strength training programs for Olympic-distance triathlons take a little more time to plan because they are approximately twice as long as sprint-distance plans. This is quite good for the athlete who likes to spend more time adapting to a particular intensity of training before changing it up. In addition, the increase in percent 1RM from one microcycle to the next is smaller, so increases in weight are not as great a shock to the body. Finally, more mesocycles can be included, so more physiological goals can be focused on, although you do have the option of using only 2 mesocycles and goals if you like. Table 7.6

**TABLE 7.6** Olympic-distance periodization plan

**Emphasis:** Swimming and running—muscular endurance, hypertrophy, and strength

**Order:** Hard to easy

Macrocycle: 12 weeks

| Mesocycle 1: 6 weeks | | | | Mesocycle 2: 4 weeks | | Mesocycle 3: 2 weeks | |
|---|---|---|---|---|---|---|---|
| Muscular endurance | | | | Hypertrophy | | Strength | |
| Week 1 | Week 2 | Weeks 3–4 | Weeks 5–6 | Weeks 1–2 | Weeks 3–4 | Week 1 | Week 2 |
| 55% 1RM | 57% 1RM | 60% 1RM | 65% 1RM | 70% 1RM | 80% 1RM | 85% 1RM | 95% 1RM |
| 2 sets | 2 sets | 2 sets | 2 sets | 3 sets | 3 sets | 4 sets | 6 sets |
| 20 rep | 18 reps | 16 reps | 14 reps | 10 reps | 8 reps | 6 reps | 2 reps |

Complete all sets of each exercise before moving to next exercise. Rest 30 seconds between sets.

**Exercises:**
Dips
Squat
Slam dunk
Leg press
Hammer curl
Lying leg curl
Bridging pullover
Cable hip flex
Seated toe raise

Complete one set of each exercise in the circuit, then repeat until all three sets are done. Rest between exercises equals the time it takes to get to the next exercise.

**Exercises:**
Squat
DB shoulder press
Upright row
Leg extension
Cable toe raise
Tubing kickback

Complete all sets of each exercise before moving to next exercise. Rest 90 seconds between sets.

**Exercises:**
Squat
Leg extension
Lying leg curl
Seated calf raise
Lateral raise
Triceps push-down
Shrugs
Retraction

illustrates a sample 12-week periodization plan that uses 3 mesocycles of differing lengths, with microcycles varying in length, intensity, and number of exercises. However, a periodized plan does not have to be this complicated. You can use the same length of time for each mesocycle and microcycle and the same number of exercises in each.

TABLE
**7.7**

**Half-Iron to Iron-distance periodization plan**

**Emphasis:** Swim, bike, and run–muscular endurance, hypertrophy, and strength

**Order:** Goal oriented by event (swim before bike before run)–add exercises as your training requires

Macrocycle: 6 months

| Mesocycle 1: 14 weeks Muscular endurance | | | | | | Mesocycle 2: 6 weeks Hypertrophy | | Mesocycle 3: 4 weeks Strength | |
|---|---|---|---|---|---|---|---|---|---|
| 3 weeks | 3 weeks | 2 weeks | 2 weeks | 2 weeks | 2 weeks | 3 weeks | 3 weeks | 2 weeks | 2 weeks |
| 55% 1RM | 58% 1RM | 61% 1RM | 63% 1RM | 65% 1RM | 67% 1RM | 72% 1RM | 79% 1RM | 85% 1RM | 88% 1RM |
| 3 sets | 3 sets | 3 sets | 2 sets | 2 sets | 2 sets | 3 sets | 3 sets | 4 sets | 4 sets |
| 20 reps | 18 reps | 16 reps | 20 reps | 18 reps | 16 reps | 10 reps | 8 reps | 5 reps | 4 reps |

## HALF-IRON TO IRON DISTANCE

Long-distance triathlons take the most toll on the body's energy and muscular systems. Although muscular endurance is key to completing this, distance, strength, power, and hypertrophy have a place as well. Remember that you can either train for more muscular endurance or make your muscles bigger and then make those larger muscles stronger and more powerful, which will provide you with more endurance. Periodization is the best way to prepare for long-distance triathlons. Circuits built within a periodized program are part of the game plan, but the overall change in goals and training emphasis really prepares you for the event. Table 7.7 is a sample plan for a 6-month strength training program. Because you probably won't do more than 2 long-distance triathlons in a season, you can spend more time preparing for each. Six months is really about the longest program you can design without a lot of guesswork, because beyond 6 months it is difficult to estimate what you will be capable of doing. The key to a successful long-term periodization plan is the testing. Initially, you must determine what your 1RM is for each exercise. Approximately halfway through the program, retest again and adjust the weights you are using. This will keep the stimulus accurate and your results coming.

---

The key to a successful long-term periodization plan is the testing.

---

Because this type of program is all-inclusive and can involve many different exercises, you can make each microcycle completely different from previous cycles. You can vary which exercises you use and how many you use, depending on how your cardio training is coming along. You only have to define the cycles, intensities, and sets or reps initially, then add the exercises as you go along. Remember that you really need to include as many as possible, if not all, of the different exercises to ensure that you cover every muscle group in every event and motion possible.

Finally, be prepared to stop and rewrite a program somewhere along the way. If you are unable to keep up with the increasing intensity and need more time in any single microcycle, that's just fine—adjust the rest of the program and keep going. The ability to make changes midstream is important to long-term planning. If you aren't flexible, you won't be able to sustain the level of training that you prescribed for yourself, and your performance will suffer.

# PART III

# Exercises

# 8

# Exercises for
# Core Conditioning

**C**ore conditioning focuses on everything except your arms, legs, and head. Although you may move these body parts during core exercises, they won't be the main muscle groups getting a workout. *Core* has been defined as the abdominal muscles, abs, and lower back, but in fact it is the part of your body to which everything is attached and from which every movement is controlled—that is, your entire torso. Whether you are putting on your running shoes, climbing into the pool, or riding your bike, your core muscles are involved.

Core conditioning is sometimes referred to as "functional training" because it involves working muscles that help you move the rest of your body. The "surface" muscles—those you can see in the mirror—are mostly responsible for the large movements; the following chapters cover them in detail. The "deep" core muscles help stabilize and control the surface muscles so that everything works together. Your core must be solid; otherwise you will use more energy to produce less powerful movements.

This chapter focuses on a few of the many exercises that target the core. They were picked specifically because they work a lot of muscle very fast and very hard, in a manner that builds the best base for the triathlon-specific exercises in later chapters.

Unlike many of the other exercises in this book, these core exercises include specific recommendations for reps and sets. Core exercises do not use much external weight, and only a few use resistance tubing, so you don't have to calculate what percent 1RM to use. For those exercises that do require a resistance tube, use one that allows you to complete the recommended reps and sets with enough resistance to make it challenging. The remainder of the exercises use body weight only and are designed to train primarily for muscular endurance. Finally, these exercises do not focus on a single muscle group; each works the entire core, but in a different way, so the results from each exercise are different.

## POINTER

**GOAL:**
**5 reps (30 seconds) each side**

Get down on your hands and knees, placing your hands directly under your shoulders and your knees directly under your hips. Press into your palms and keep a slight bend in your elbows. Your hands should be no more than shoulder width apart and your knees no more than hip width apart. Before starting any motion, your back must be in a neutral position

**FIGURE 8.1** Pointer start/finish position

(Figure 8.1). To achieve this, arch your back as far as possible, then allow it to sag as much as possible. The neutral position is exactly in the middle between these extremes. When you are in a neutral position, your shoulders should not feel pinched or be pressing up toward your head. Prevent this by pushing

**FIGURE 8.2** Pointer first position

**FIGURE 8.3** Pointer second position

your upper back toward the ceiling and holding it there during the exercise.

Achieve the first position by lifting one arm straight out in front of you so that you are balancing on the other hand and both knees (Figure 8.2). Hold this position until you feel stable and are not wobbling. Then raise the opposite leg straight out behind you into the second position (Figure 8.3). If your left arm is out, straighten your right leg, and vice versa. Hold this position for up to 30 seconds, or until you start to lose your balance. Lower your arm and leg and rest for 10 to 15 seconds. Repeat both positions with the other arm and leg. Your goal is to complete 5 reps of 30 seconds on each side.

GOAL:
**2 sets, 20 reps**

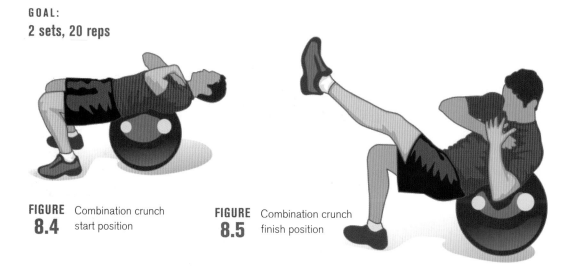

**FIGURE 8.4**  Combination crunch start position

**FIGURE 8.5**  Combination crunch finish position

Lie faceup on a stability ball so that the top of the ball is in the curve of your lower back, with your feet planted flat on the floor. Allow your body to arch backward over the ball. Lift your hips so they are at about the same height as your knees and move your feet away from the ball until they are directly under your knees. You can keep your feet close together for maximum instability (making the exercise harder), or move them apart for more stability and balance. Cross your arms over your chest with your fingers touching your shoulders (Figure 8.4). Lift your right shoulder up and across your body toward your left hip. At the same time, lift your left leg and point it out and away from you (Figure 8.5). Immediately relax back to the start position and do a rep on the other side. Alternate repetitions from side to side until you have completed 20 repetitions, then rest for 30 seconds and do another set.

**GOAL:**
**2 sets, 15 reps**

**FIGURE** V-up start position
**8.6**

Lie on your back with your feet and legs together and your arms extended over your head (Figure 8.6). Clasp your hands together so that your arms stay straight all the time.

Take a deep breath and slowly exhale while lifting your arms, upper body, and legs into the air, trying to bring them together as high as possible over your hips (Figure 8.7). When you get to the top of the movement, your entire upper body and legs should be off the floor, with only your buttocks touching it. Immediately lower yourself down slowly, trying to make your shoulders and legs reach the floor at the same time. Focus on controlling your movements and don't try to do these fast, so that the muscles will work as they should. Rest for a couple of seconds, take another deep breath, and repeat. Your goal is 2 sets of 15 reps.

**FIGURE** V-up finish position
**8.7**

**GOAL:**
**2 sets, 10 reps each side**

**FIGURE** Modified sit-up
**8.8** start/finish position

**FIGURE** Modified sit-up finish position
**8.9**

**FIGURE** Modified sit-up without anchor
**8.10**

Lie on your back with your knees bent and your feet flat on the floor. Your heels should be no more than a foot away from your buttocks. Raise a leg about 1 foot off the floor. Anchor the other leg by either putting your foot under an object or having someone hold it down (Figure 8.8). (Once you get stronger, you will be able to do this without anchoring your foot; see Figure 8.10.) Cross your arms over your chest or put your hands on the sides of your head, but don't lock your hands behind your head or support your head with your hands (this can cause neck injury).

Take a deep breath and then exhale while rolling your head and shoulders off the ground toward your knees (Figure 8.9). When your shoulders leave the floor, contract your abdominals and begin pulling with your hip flexor muscles to bring your entire back all the way off the floor. Keep moving up until you can touch an elbow to your bent knee, then slowly lower yourself back to the floor. Don't jerk up off the floor when your abs get tired because this will cause your back muscles to contract and could cause injury. Complete 10 reps on one side, then switch and do another 10 reps on the other side. Rest for 1 minute and complete a second set.

## MODIFIED BRIDGE

GOAL:
**5 reps (30 seconds) each side**

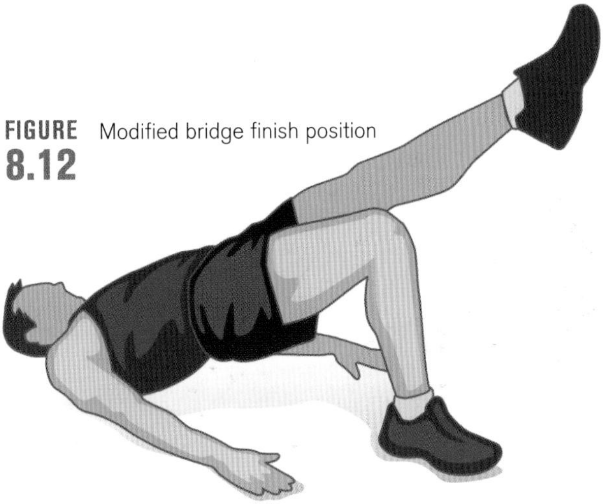

FIGURE **8.12** Modified bridge finish position

FIGURE **8.11** Modified bridge start position

Lie on your back with your knees bent and your feet flat on the floor. Your heels should be no more than 1 foot away from your buttocks. Lift a leg about 1 foot off the floor and hold it straight out. Place both arms down at your sides with your palms pressing against the floor (Figure 8.11).

In one smooth motion, lift your hips into the air until your knees, hips, and shoulders are in a straight line (Figure 8.12). Do not lift your hips so high that you can't see your knees. You may push against the floor with your hands to help lift your hips, but try not to. Hold this position for 30 seconds, then relax back to the floor and repeat with the other leg. Alternate sides until you complete 5 reps on each.

GOAL:
**5 reps (30 seconds)
each side**

**FIGURE 8.13** Back bridge start position

**FIGURE 8.14** Back bridge finish position

**FIGURE 8.15** Back bridge variation with 1 foot on the ball

Lie on your back with your knees bent and your feet flat against the top of a stability ball. Place your arms at your sides with your palms facing the floor (Figure 8.13). (When you get really good at this exercise, put your arms across your chest.)

Push on the ball with your feet to lift your hips up into the air until your body is in a straight line from your knees to your shoulders

(Figure 8.14). Hold this position for 30 seconds, then relax back to the floor, take a couple of deep breaths, and repeat for a total of 5 reps. If you want to make this exercise more difficult, hold one foot up in the air, and with the other foot in the middle of the ball, push up into the bridge position (Figure 8.15). CAUTION: If you feel any pain in your neck or cramping in your hamstrings, stop immediately and rest. Pain in the neck or back should be discusssed with your doctor before you continue.

## RUSSIAN BALL TWIST

GOAL:
**3 sets, 30 reps**

**FIGURE 8.16** Russian ball twist start position

Lie faceup on your stability ball so the ball is resting in the small of your back and your shoulders are not touching the ball. Keep your feet under your knees and hip width apart. Contract your glutes and lower back muscles to lift your hips so that your body is in a straight line from your shoulders to your knees; hold your hips in this position until the exercise is finished. Clasp your hands together and raise your arms toward the ceiling (Figure 8.16).

Keeping your feet still and your body as straight as possible, roll to your left side until your arms are pointing to your left. You should now be balancing on your left shoulder only. Roll back the other way onto your right shoulder, pointing your arms out to your right side. Only your right shoulder should be touching the ball now. Continue rolling left and right (doing both sides equals 1 rep) until you have finished 30 reps (Figure 8.17). Rest for 1 minute and complete 2 more sets. If you want to make this exercise more difficult, lift the opposite foot off the ground as you rotate from side to side (Figure 8.18) or hold a medicine ball in your hands.

**FIGURE 8.17** Russian ball twist finish position

**FIGURE 8.18** Russian ball twist variation with foot raised

**GOAL:**
**2 sets, 20 reps**

**FIGURE 8.20** Moguls left finish position

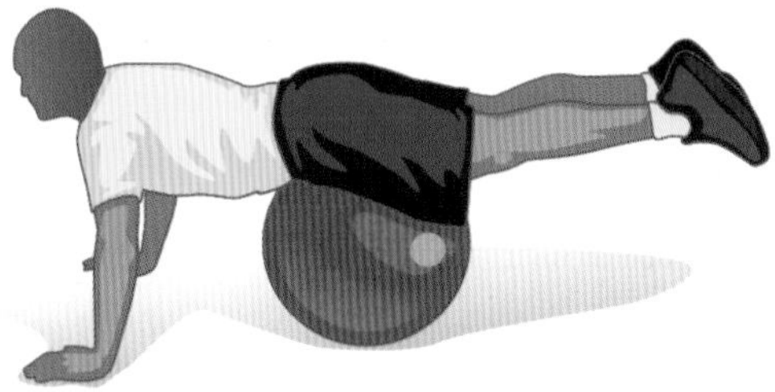

**FIGURE 8.19** Moguls start position

**FIGURE 8.21** Moguls right finish position

Lie facedown on your stability ball. Place your hands on the floor right under your shoulders and straighten your arms. Keep your knees and feet together and hold your legs straight out. Slowly "walk" out on your hands until the ball is at your hips (Figure 8.19). Hold yourself in this position and keep the ball from moving side to side.

Using your arms to hold your upper body in place, bring your knees up toward your chest and at the same time rotate your hips so that your legs move out to your left side and your right leg is the only part of you touching the ball (Figure 8.20). Straighten back out to the starting position by rolling your legs back under you and

on your hip (Figure 8.25). Facing away from the anchor point, move away from the anchor until all the slack is out of the tubing. Stand with your feet shoulder width apart. The foot on the same side as the hand holding the tubing should be slightly behind the other foot for a good, stable base.

Push your hand away from your body as if you were punching someone in slow motion. At the same time, rotate your body so that the hand with the tubing in it can reach as far in front of you as possible. Rotate your body as far as you can, pushing out on the tubing. When you get to the finish position (Figure 8.26), slowly return to the start position, making sure your hand ends up next to your shoulder, where it started. Repeat for 15 reps, then switch sides; complete 2 sets on each side.

# 9

# Upper-Body Exercises
# for Swimming

The ability of your arms to pull and push your body through water is a huge part of successful swimming. The pull begins when the hand enters the water and you "pull" it toward your chest. The push occurs at the point where your hand passes your shoulder and starts moving toward your hip. Unfortunately, there aren't any exercise machines that mimic swimming strokes. The good news is that with a little creativity, you can target the individual muscles used during any stroke, and by combining several exercises you can work all the upper-body muscles involved in swimming. Some of these exercises focus on the stroke itself; others focus on the recovery. For those exercises that use resistance tubing, the proper number of repetitions per set has been provided, but you can choose the proper number of sets and amount of rest between sets for your own goal.

Upper-body strength training for swimming focuses on the deltoid muscles of the shoulder, which work during all of the stroke movement; the latissimus dorsi (lats) and biceps for the pull of the stroke; and the triceps for the push of the stroke.

**MUSCLE FOCUS:**
**Lats and deltoids**

**FIGURE
9.1** One-arm throw
start position

**FIGURE
9.2** One-arm throw
finish position

The one-arm throw focuses on the front portion of your deltoid muscles and on your lats, in a motion that simulates how your upper arm pulls you through the water.

Loop your resistance tubing through a door anchor at the top of a door or around a pole above your head. Hold 1 handle in 1 hand, or for more resistance, hold both handles in 1 hand. Facing away from the anchor, hold your arm over your head and step away until there is no slack in the tubing and it is just starting to pull you backward. Balance on the leg on the same side as the arm holding the tubing (Figure 9.1).

Keeping your body upright and still and your arm perfectly straight, quickly pull down on the tubing until your arm is pointing out in front of you (Figure 9.2), then quickly return it to the starting point. You should be moving with some speed, but don't let the tubing "bounce" back and forth—always be in control of it. Repeat 10 to 15 times on that side, then switch sides to complete your set.

## SLAM DUNK

**MUSCLE FOCUS:**
**Lats, deltoids, and triceps**

**FIGURE 9.3** Slam dunk start position

**FIGURE 9.4** Slam dunk finish position

The slam dunk is all about creating powerful strokes and moving your arm from over your head through a full range of motion down to your side. You won't use both arms at the same time to pull during swimming, but using them together now allows you to get more out of the exercise than using 1 arm would.

Stand with your feet about shoulder width apart. Hold a 10- to 15-pound medicine ball in both hands over your head as high as you can reach (Figure 9.3). Keep a firm grasp on both sides of the ball; you are going to throw it down.

With lots of power and speed, bring the ball down toward the floor directly in front of you. Release the ball once it gets to about hip level, before you start bending at the hips (Figure 9.4). If the ball you are using bounces, it should bounce right back up into your hands. Catch it and let the momentum carry you back to the start position. If the ball doesn't bounce, quickly bend down, pick it up, and lift it back to the start position. When you get the ball back over your head, slam it down again. Repeat slam dunks for 10 to 15 reps per set.

## BRIDGING PULLOVER

**MUSCLE FOCUS:**
**Lats and deltoids**

The bridging pullover focuses on a powerful pull, with the added effect of an unstable torso, using a stability ball. This exercise will help you learn to pull stronger while keeping your body from moving around too much.

Loop your resistance tubing through your door anchor or around a pole at hip level. Hold one handle in each hand. If this is too much resistance, anchor one end of the tubing and hold the other end in

**FIGURE 9.5** Bridging pullover start position

**FIGURE 9.6** Bridging pullover
finish position

both hands. Sit on your stability ball facing away from the anchor. Holding your arms over your head, lie back on the ball faceup, letting it roll up your back until your shoulders are on top of the ball. Your arms should now be pointing back behind you toward the tubing anchor (Figure 9.5). Hold your hips up in the bridging position so that your knees, hips, and shoulders are in a straight line and your back is straight. If there is any slack in the tubing, sit up and move farther away from the anchor.

Keeping your body in the bridging position, pull the tubing up over your head and then down, until your arms are pointing out in front of you (Figure 9.6). Keep your arms completely straight during the entire pull. If you need to raise your head to see where you are pointing, that's fine. Slowly return to the start position while staying in control of the tubing—don't let it pull you back too fast. As you get better at this exercise, you will be able to do it faster and with more power. Do 10 to 15 reps per set.

**MUSCLE FOCUS:**
**Lats, deltoids,**
**biceps, and triceps**

The tubing stroke is a complete pull-and-push maneuver, exactly what you do while swimming. Everyone has a slightly different stroke style, and this exercise allows you to mimic your own style, with the resistance tubing trying to pull your arm back over your head.

Loop your resistance tubing through a door anchor at the top of the door or around a pole above your head. Kneel on the floor, facing the tubing anchor. Hold one end of the tubing in each hand and lift your arms above your head (Figure 9.7). There should be no slack in the tubing at the start position; to get rid of slack, either loop the tubing through the anchor again to shorten it or wrap the tubing around your hands to shorten it.

**FIGURE 9.7** Tubing stroke start position

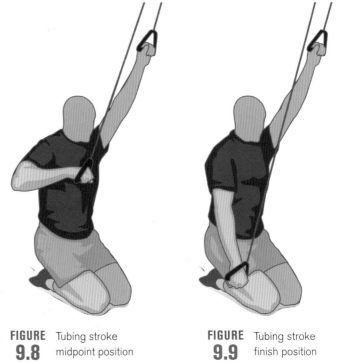

**FIGURE 9.8** Tubing stroke midpoint position

**FIGURE 9.9** Tubing stroke finish position

The goal of this exercise is to mimic your personal swimming stroke, so the movement will be different for everybody. Using 1 hand at a time, pull the tubing down with your normal stroke movement (Figure 9.8); once it passes the level of your elbow, push it all the way down to finish the stroke (Figure 9.9). Concentrate on moving in your normal stroke pattern, not just on getting your hand down. Let your arm return to the starting position, controlling the movement (don't let the tubing yank your arm back up). Now complete a stroke on the other side. Alternate left and right arms until you have completed 20 to 30 total strokes per set.

## DB SHOULDER PRESS

**MUSCLE FOCUS:**
**Deltoids and triceps**

**FIGURE 9.10** DB shoulder press start position

The DB shoulder press is designed to help you straighten out your arm completely prior to beginning a stroke. In the water you won't have as much resistance as the dumbbells provide, so actual swimming will be much easier than this exercise.

**FIGURE 9.11**  DB shoulder press finish position

Sit on top of your stability ball with your feet spread apart on the floor, slightly wider than your shoulders. Sit up as straight as you can during the entire exercise. Hold a dumbbell in each hand at shoulder level, either in front of or just to the sides of your shoulders (Figure 9.10), whichever is more comfortable for you. Your palms can be facing away from or toward you.

Push both dumbbells over your head at the same time until your arms are completely straight. The dumbbells will naturally move closer together as you push up, and they can touch at the very top of the press (Figure 9.11). As you press them up, think about trying to move them in a straight line from your shoulders to directly over your head. Don't let them sway forward or backward, as this wastes energy and means you aren't in control of them. Slowly lower the dumbbells back to the start position. If this exercise is difficult for you, have a spotter stand behind you to make sure you don't drop a dumbbell.

The triceps push-down concentrates on the last half of your stroke, the push. The relatively small triceps muscles have to provide the last push to propel you through the water, so training them is essential.

Attach a straight or V-shaped handle to a high-pulley cable machine. (This provides the best technique for this exercise.) Grasp the handle so your hands are evenly spaced from the middle to prevent tilting. Using a relaxed overhand (palms facing down) grip, bend your elbows so the handles come as close to your shoulders as possible and bring your elbows to your sides (Figure 9.12). Stand as close to the cable as possible without pushing it away from you. If you find that the handle is swinging away from you during the exercise, take a small step back. Move your feet apart, with one foot in front of the other for good balance.

Keeping your elbows at your sides, push down on the handle until both arms are completely straight (Figure 9.13). Slowly let your elbows bend to bring the handle back to the start position. During the entire movement, your elbows should remain at your sides—only your forearms and hands should be moving. If you want a bigger challenge, do this exercise 1 arm at a time using a single-hand attachment.

**MUSCLE FOCUS:**
**Triceps**

**FIGURE 9.12** Triceps push-down start position

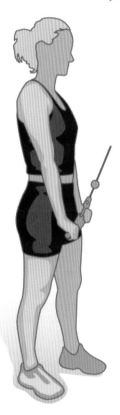

**FIGURE 9.13** Triceps push-down finish position

**MUSCLE FOCUS:**
**Triceps**

**FIGURE 9.14** Tubing kickback start position

**FIGURE 9.15** Tubing kickback finish position

The tubing kickback also mimics the final push of your stroke, but with just 1 hand at a time.

Attach 1 end of your resistance tubing to your door anchor, or loop it around a pole at chest level and hold the other end of the tubing in one hand. Place the free hand on your thigh. Bend forward slightly at the hips, keeping your back straight. Bend the arm holding the tubing, lifting your elbow up until your upper arm is parallel to the floor (your shoulder and elbow should be at the same height) (Figure 9.14). Keep your hand as close to your shoulder as possible. Now back up until there is some stretch and resistance in the tubing.

Concentrate on keeping your body, elbow, and shoulder still as you straighten out your arm behind you, pulling the tubing out. Pull on the tubing until your arm is pointing completely straight behind you (Figure 9.15). Slowly let your elbow bend again, bringing your hand back to your shoulder. Don't let the tubing control the movement and snap back too quickly. Do 10 to 15 reps, then switch sides.

## DIPS

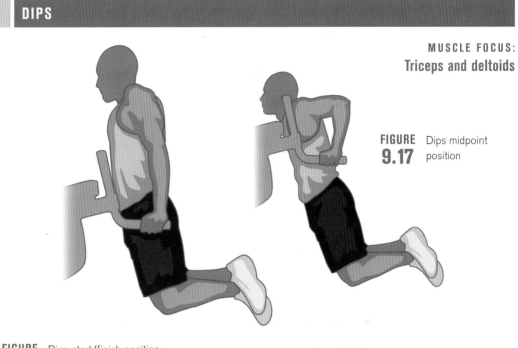

MUSCLE FOCUS:
**Triceps and deltoids**

**FIGURE 9.17**  Dips midpoint position

**FIGURE 9.16**  Dips start/finish position

The dip is one of the most difficult but useful exercises in this book. It combines extension of the elbow from the triceps with flexion of the shoulder from the deltoid to double the force of your push.

Use a dip stand specially made for doing this exercise. A dip stand is sometimes combined with a knee raise stand or a pull-up stand. The arms of the stand usually are not adjustable, but if they are, adjust them so that they are just wider than your hips. Use the steps provided to get up to the start position. Place a hand on each of the dip stand arms, palms facing toward your body. It's best to grasp the bar with your thumb on one side and your fingers on the other so your hand can't slip off during the exercise. Press yourself up until your arms are completely straight, holding your body up unsupported (you have to step off the stand now). Cross your feet at your ankles and bend your knees so you don't touch the floor at the midpoint of this exercise (Figure 9.16).

Slowly bend your elbows and lower yourself toward the floor until your shoulders and elbows are at the same level and your upper arms are parallel to the floor (Figure 9.17). Once you have reached this position, push with both hands to straighten your arms until your elbows are perfectly straight again and you are back at the start position.

**FIGURE 9.18**  Seated dips start/finish position

**FIGURE 9.19**  Seated dips midpoint position

If you don't have a dip stand or find this exercise too difficult, you can use a flat bench and do a variation of the dip called the seated dip (although you never really sit down). For this variation, with your back to a bench, place your hands on the edge, palms facing away from you, and slide your legs straight out in front of you until you have made a "bridge" of your body (Figure 9.18). Slowly let your elbows and hips bend as if you were going to sit on the floor. Keep lowering yourself until your shoulders and elbows are at the same height and your upper arms are parallel to the floor (Figure 9.19). Then push on your hands to straighten back up. If you end up sitting on the floor, find a taller bench.

## DB CURL

**MUSCLE FOCUS:**
**Biceps**

If you watch how your arm moves during the initial pull of your stroke, you will notice that the elbow has to bend to keep your hand close to your body. The biceps make this possible, and without them your pull would be very weak.

Hold a dumbbell in each hand using an underhand grip (palms facing front). Stand with your feet shoulder width apart and your knees slightly bent, letting the dumbbells rest against the outsides of your thighs (Figure 9.20). Your arms should be completely straight.

To prevent swaying your back, perform the DB curl 1 arm at a time, alternating hands. Slowly bend your elbow and bring the dumbbell up to shoulder height (Figure 9.21). When

**FIGURE 9.20** DB curl start position

**FIGURE 9.21** DB curl finish position

curling, keep your elbow at your side so the only part of your body that is moving is your forearm and hand. Slowly lower the dumbbell until your arm is completely straight again. Alternate left and right curls until your set is complete.

# 10

# Lower-Body Exercises for Swimming

**A**lthough the upper body may be the powerhouse during swimming, the lower body provides a good deal of propulsion and stability in the water. During your swim training you probably do drills that focus on just the upper or lower body, which is why you need to do strength training that focuses on each part as well. The lower body, which includes your hips, thighs, and calves, doesn't provide a lot of buoyancy, so you have to keep it moving during the swim to prevent dragging your legs along at the expense of your arms. Strength training for the lower body won't provide a huge increase in your swimming speed or performance, but you will see its effects when you transition to the bike and run, where your legs are most important. If your legs are not strong in the water, they will be tired when the swim is finished and won't be able to move you as fast on the bike and run.

Lower-body strength training for swimming focuses on the glute muscles (gluteus maximus and medius), which extend your hips to the back and side; the hamstrings, which help with hip extension; the adductor group, which is responsible for keeping your legs close to your body; the quadriceps, which are strong knee extensors and hip flexors; and the calves, which point the feet and toes.

## CABLE LATERAL LIFT

**MUSCLE FOCUS:**
**Gluteus medius**

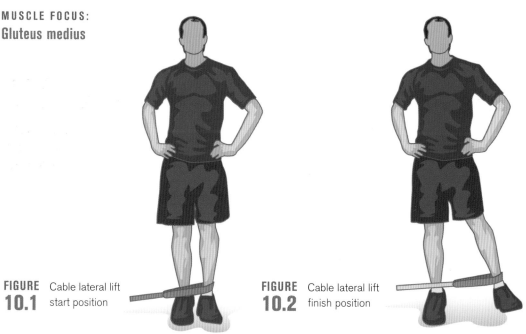

**FIGURE 10.1** Cable lateral lift start position

**FIGURE 10.2** Cable lateral lift finish position

The cable lateral lift focuses on the often-ignored smaller glute muscle— the gluteus medius. This muscle is responsible for lifting your legs out to your sides and for stabilizing the larger gluteus medius during hip extension. Training this muscle will help keep your legs from flailing out to the sides and allow you to concentrate on extending your hips with each kick.

Attach the ankle strap of a low-pulley machine to one leg. Stand so that the leg you are going to work is farthest away from the machine and the cable crosses in front of you. Hold on to the machine with 1 hand and place the other hand on your hip, or place both hands on your hips (Figure 10.1).

Keep your body as straight as possible while you lift your leg directly out to the side as high as you can (Figure 10.2). Concentrate on moving your leg to the side and not forward or backward. If you start to lean your upper body toward the machine, that's as high as you can go; leaning doesn't work the glute muscles. Slowly bring your leg back down and repeat until your set is complete, then switch sides and do a set for the other leg.

## INCLINED SUPERMAN

**MUSCLE FOCUS:**
**Gluteus maximus and hamstrings**

**FIGURE 10.3** Inclined Superman start position

**FIGURE 10.4** Inclined Superman finish position

The inclined Superman locks your knees straight while you use your glutes and hamstrings to extend your hips. By keeping your knees locked, you are able to make the hamstrings work at the hips, effectively increasing the force of hip extension during your kick.

Facing away from a wall, lie facedown over your stability ball. Anchor your feet by setting your toes on the floor and your heels against the wall. Keep your legs straight. Position the ball so that the top of it is at your waist and your head is lower than your hips. Hold your arms straight out over your head (Figure 10.3).

Take a deep breath, then exhale as you roll your back up until your body is straight. Continue to tighten your glutes until you have lifted your upper body as high as you can (Figure 10.4). Your upper legs and hips will stay on the ball. Really focus on squeezing your glutes, and if you feel this in your lower back, that's normal—those muscles are supporting your upper body. Slowly relax back to the start position, then repeat for 10 to 15 times per set. If you need more resistance, hold a medicine ball in your hands.

## LEG EXTENSION

**MUSCLE FOCUS:**
**Quadriceps**

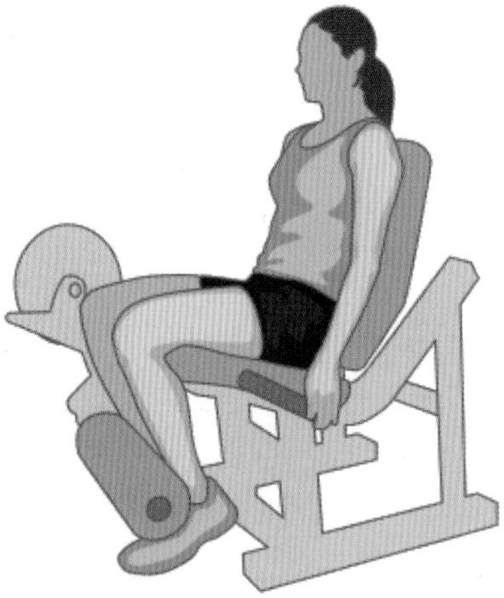

**FIGURE 10.5** Leg extension start position

The leg extension machine has a bad rap as an exercise that will hurt your knees. The evidence for this is minimal and usually involves people who have had a previous knee injury. If your knees hurt, don't do this exercise, but if they are healthy, performing it correctly should not cause any damage. This exercise concentrates on the force

that you produce while extending your knees, which is critical for a solid kick.

Sit down on the leg extension machine and adjust the seat back so that your knees line up with the machine's pivot point. The pivot point is always evident (or can be found on the machine's instruction card) and is usually at the edge of the seat. If your knees are too far forward, there will be a lot of strain on them at the start of the exercise. Place your feet behind the footpad and adjust it so the pad rests just above your feet on your shins (Figure 10.5). (Some machines adjust themselves, so you may not have to do this.) If you can adjust how far under the seat the leg pad is, move it so that you start with your knees bent at about a 90-degree angle. Too great an angle at the start can cause knee pain, especially if you have had a knee injury. If your knees hurt at all during this exercise, skip it and use another exercise.

Holding on to the handles, straighten out your legs as far as possible. The goal is to get your legs completely extended (Figure 10.6). Slowly lower your legs back down to a point just before the weight stack comes to a rest, then repeat until your set is complete.

**MUSCLE FOCUS:**
**Gluteus maximus and hamstrings**

**FIGURE 10.7** Cable hip extension start position

**FIGURE 10.8** Cable hip extension finish position

The cable hip extension exercise allows you to work 1 leg at a time through the same range of motion that the hips move during swimming. You can alter the range of motion you use here to fit you best.

Attach the ankle strap of a low-pulley machine to one leg. Stand facing the machine and hold on to the machine with both hands. Step back until your arms are straight and there is just a little pull on the cable. Put all your weight on your support leg (the one without the ankle strap) and keep your body as upright as possible (Figure 10.7).

Keeping your leg straight, push it back as far as you can (Figure 10.8). This is not a large motion, so focus on squeezing your glutes tight. You may be tempted to lean your body forward to get more range of motion, but this actually decreases the effectiveness of the exercise, so stay standing straight. Slowly return to the start position, then repeat until your set is complete.

122 | STRENGTH TRAINING FOR TRIATHLETES

## CABLE LATERAL CROSS

The adductor muscles used during the cable lateral cross exercise are responsible for helping the gluteus medius stabilize the hips and the gluteus maximus. Performing this exercise will also help with your hip extension force by keeping the leg moving in the correct direction.

Attach the ankle strap of a low-pulley machine to one leg. Stand so that the leg you are going to work is closest to the machine. Place both hands on your hips and step away from the machine until your working leg is being pulled toward it (Figure 10.9). Put all your weight on the other leg. If you feel off balance, place a chair in front of you to hold on to.

Pull your extended leg back toward your support leg and then across in front of you as far as possible (Figure 10.10). Slowly return back to the start position, then repeat until your set is complete. As you move, make sure that the only part of you that is moving is your leg. Don't let your shoulders or hips turn toward the machine in an effort to move your leg farther.

**FIGURE 10.10** Cable lateral cross finish position

**FIGURE 10.9** Cable lateral cross start position

**MUSCLE FOCUS:**
**Hamstrings**

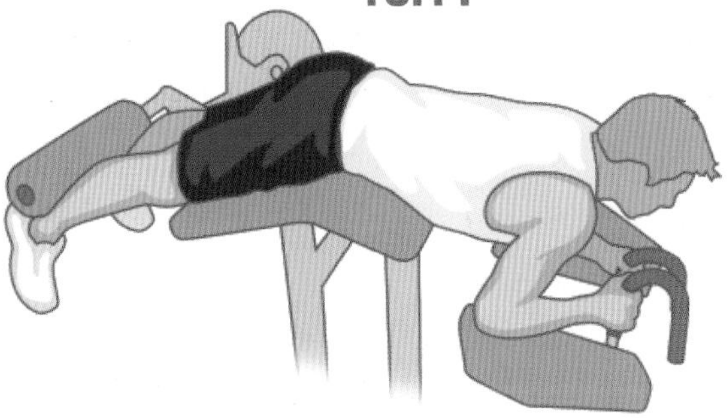

**FIGURE** Lying leg curl start position
**10.11**

FIGURE Lying leg curl start position
10.11

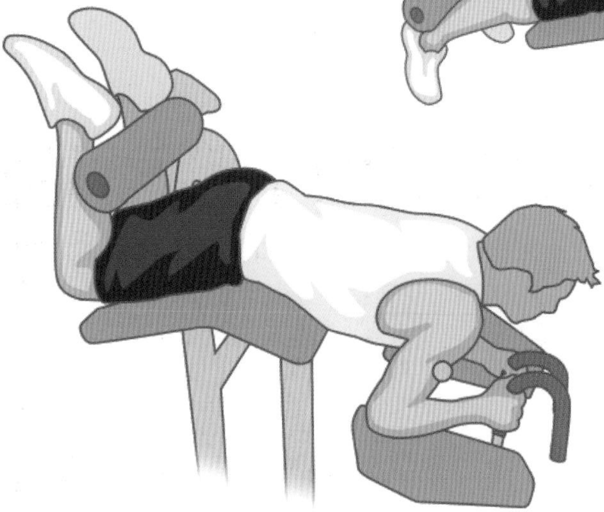

FIGURE Lying leg curl finish position
10.12

The lying leg curl mimics the position of swimming better than other leg curl exercises.

Find the pivot point of the lying leg curl machine. Usually it is right at the edge of the padding. Stand at the end of the bench with your knees right against the padding and lie facedown. Your kneecaps should hang off the end of the bench and line up with the machine pivot point. Lie all the way down and hold on to the handles. (Some machines have pads for your elbows to rest on; others have a flat bench to rest your chest and head on. Either is fine.) Your feet should be underneath the leg pad (Figure 10.11). Some machines adjust this automatically, but if yours does not, adjust the pad so it is in contact with the back of your shins (on your Achilles tendon) and is not pushing on your foot.

Bend your knees, pulling the footpad up as far as you can (Figure 10.12). The goal is to get the pad all the way to your buttocks. The farther you can "curl" your legs, the more you get out of this exercise. Try to keep your hips flat on the pad during the motion. If they start to rise, hold them down by tightening your glutes. Slowly let your legs back down until the weights almost touch, then repeat until your set is complete.

## SEATED CALF RAISE

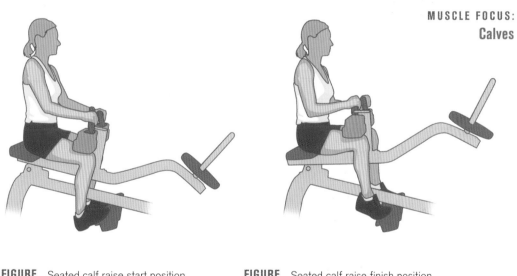

MUSCLE FOCUS:
Calves

**FIGURE 10.13** Seated calf raise start position

**FIGURE 10.14** Seated calf raise finish position

The seated calf raise makes the soleus muscle in your calf work most. This muscle is a very strong endurance-oriented muscle that keeps your feet pointed while swimming.

Sit down on the machine and place your feet on the footplate so that just the balls of your feet are on the plate and your heels are hanging off the back. Slide your knees under the pads, and adjust the knee pads so they are snug against your knees but not pushing down hard (Figure 10.13). You can hold on to the hand grips, but make sure not to pull the knee pad up with your hands during the exercise—that job must be done by your calves.

Push on the balls of your feet to raise your heels as high as you can (Figure 10.14). On the first rep, the bar that supports the machine will move out of the way. Lower your heels as far as you can to get a good stretch. When you can't go down anymore, push back up on the balls of your feet to get back to the highest point you can reach. Repeat, lowering and raising your heels until you have finished all your reps. On the last rep, when you are at the highest point, move the support bar back under the machine and lower the bar back down on it.

## STANDING CALF RAISE

**MUSCLE FOCUS:**
**Calves**

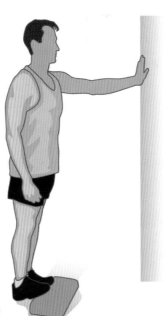

**FIGURE 10.15** Standing calf raise start position

In the standing calf raise you will work both the soleus and the gastrocnemius muscles of the calf. The gastrocnemius muscle provides more power to your kick and helps the soleus.

Stand straight with your legs together. You can do this exercise standing flat on the floor, but by standing on the edge of a step, curb, aerobics bench, or even a piece of wood, you will get a larger range of motion and better results. If you use a step, stand on the very edge of it so just the balls of your feet are on it, and let your heels hang over the edge (Figure 10.15). Hold on to something in front of you for support.

Let your heels drop as far toward the floor as possible, then push up on the balls of your feet until you can't go any higher (Figure 10.16). Be sure both legs are pushing as much as they can—don't let 1 leg do all the work. Slowly lower your heels back toward the floor and repeat until your set is finished.

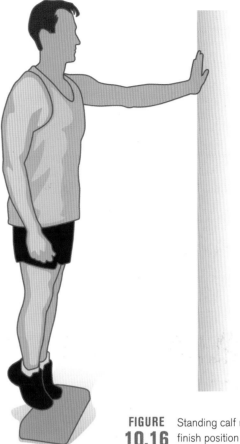

**FIGURE 10.16** Standing calf raise finish position

# 11

# Upper-Body Exercises
# for Cycling

In the past the focus of strength training for cycling has been on the legs, which makes sense because the legs were assumed to provide all the propulsion. However, a study of basic biomechanics shows that although the legs do push the pedals and turn the crank, they are able to do so only if the upper body provides a base to push against. For example, think of how much power you produce, or how hard you can ride, when you are in your normal riding position, compared with how hard you can ride when you aren't holding the handlebars at all. The amount of force you can produce always drops when you let go of the bars because your base of support is gone. It does not require a huge amount of strength to provide this support; merely holding the bars is usually enough, until your legs start to fade, then the upper body starts to work harder.

In addition, your upper body must support the weight of your torso as you lean over the handlebars, whether in a traditional or an aerobar position. Your lower body is supported by the seat, but the bulk of the work of holding your upper body is done by the arms, shoulders, and back. Increasing the performance of these muscles in cycling-specific exercises will decrease your fatigue during cycling and give you more energy during the run.

This chapter focuses on the upper-body muscles—collectively called the erector spinae, upper back muscles (trapezius, rhomboids), shoulders (deltoids), chest (pectoralis major, or pecs), triceps, and wrist flexors.

## BACK EXTENSION

**MUSCLE FOCUS:**
**Erector spinae,**
**rhomboids, and**
**trapezius**

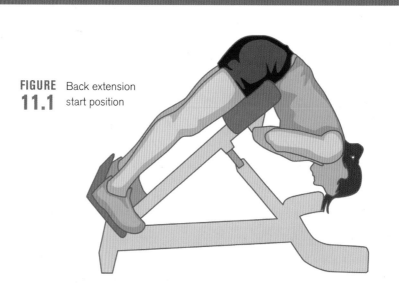

**FIGURE** Back extension
**11.1** start position

The back extension exercise is the only one that focuses on the erector spinae muscles, which are responsible for keeping your back straight. As these muscles tire, you start to slouch, which puts additional strain on the rest of your body. Keeping your back straight while cycling helps with aerodynamics and prevents a tight back later, during the run.

Using a 45-degree back extension bench, adjust the height of the thigh pad so that it is just below your waist and allows you to fully

**FIGURE**
**11.2** Back extension halfway-up position

**FIGURE**
**11.3** Back extension finish position

bend over without pressing into your stomach. Mount the bench, making sure your heels are set against the heel pads or heel plate that locks your legs so that you don't fall off. Your legs should remain straight during the exercise, but you may turn your toes out to the sides to relieve the pressure on your thighs. Cross your arms over your chest and slowly lower yourself over the bench by bending at the waist (Figure 11.1). The goal is to get as far down as you can, so really relax your back and shoulder muscles.

Starting with your lower back, slowly roll yourself up by moving one vertebra at a time, the way a cat arches its back (Figure 11.2). Do not try to hold your back flat or straight. Your shoulders should be the last part of your back that unrolls. It will take some practice to activate these small muscles individually. Roll up to the point at which your body is in a straight line (Figure 11.3)—any farther is hyperextension of the spine, which is undesirable.

**MUSCLE FOCUS:**
**Pecs and deltoids**

**FIGURE** Protraction start position
**11.4**

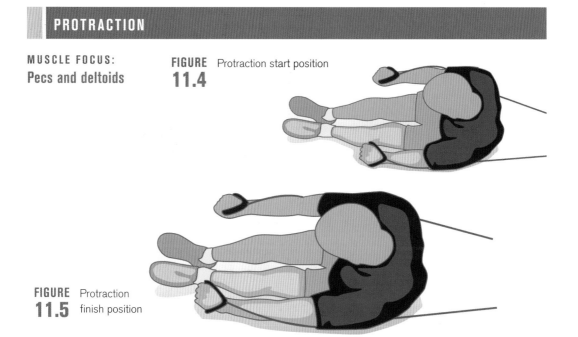

**FIGURE** Protraction
**11.5** finish position

Protraction is a very small movement, but it is very important for keeping your upper back and shoulders in a strong position during your ride. The pecs and front portion of the deltoids work together to pull your shoulders forward, effectively pushing your back into a straight position and keeping your shoulders from tiring.

Attach a resistance tube to an anchor or wrap it around a pole a couple of feet off the floor. Sit on the floor facing away from the anchor, holding one end of the resistance tubing in each hand. Straighten your arms out in front of you and relax your shoulders to let the tubing pull your arms and shoulders back (Figure 11.4).

Push out on the tubing handles, bringing your shoulders as far forward as possible (Figure 11.5). Hold yourself still; don't lean forward to move the handles. This exercise takes only about 4 to 6 inches of movement, and it all has to come from the shoulders. Now let your shoulders be pulled back again, fully relax them, and repeat until your set is finished.

## FRONT RAISE

**FIGURE 11.6** Front raise start position

**FIGURE 11.7** Front raise finish position

The front raise is designed to make sure your shoulders are strong enough to hold your body up while on your bike. The shoulders are in the weakest joint position when you are bent over the handlebars, because they have to bear the brunt of your upper-body weight and keep you in an upright position.

Stand with your feet slightly apart, with 1 foot in front of the other for a stable stance (doesn't matter which foot is in front). Hold a dumbbell in each hand, with your palms facing your legs (Figure 11.6). Slowly lift 1 dumbbell straight out in front of you until it is at shoulder height (Figure 11.7). Your arm should remain as straight as possible the entire time. Slowly lower the dumbbell back to your leg, then repeat with the other arm, alternating until you have completed all your reps.

## DB HANDLE PUSH-UP

**MUSCLE FOCUS:**
Pecs, triceps,
and deltoids

**FIGURE 11.8** DB handle push-up start position

**FIGURE 11.9** DB handle push-up finish position

The DB handle push-up takes a regular push-up and gives it more range of motion, so that the shoulders, chest, and triceps work more. Sometimes during a ride, especially while facing a strong headwind, you may drop your body lower over the handlebars to create a more aerodynamic position. This exercise helps you hold that position and then push back up out of it when you need to.

Place a pair of dumbbells on the floor in front of you. Get down on your hands and knees and grab the dumbbell handles, positioning them so they line up across your body (perpendicular to you), your palms facing your knees, and your hands directly under your shoulders. The farther apart your hands are, the less effective and sport-specific this exercise becomes. Stretch out your legs behind you and put your feet next to each other or no more than a couple

**FIGURE 11.10** DB handle push-up modified start position

**FIGURE 11.11** DB handle push-up modified finish position

of inches apart (Figure 11.8). Your toes should be the only part of your body touching the ground. If you have trouble completing a push-up in this position, you can do a modified push-up on your knees rather than your toes (Figure 11.10). In either case, keep your body rigid and maintain a straight line with your shoulders, hips, and feet (Figure 11.9) (or shoulders, hips, and knees in the modified position; see Figure 11.11). Don't let your hips sag, and don't stick your buttocks up in the air—your entire body must move together and be straight as a board.

Slowly lower yourself toward the floor by bending your arms until either your chest comes in contact with the floor or your shoulders are lower than your elbows. Don't go down so far that you are lying on the floor—just get close and then push yourself back to the start position. It helps to breathe in as you lower yourself and breathe out as you push back up.

This is a body weight–only exercise. Do not attempt to make it more difficult by placing weights on your back. If you want to make it harder, wear a proper weighted vest or just do more reps.

**MUSCLE FOCUS:**
**Wrist flexors**
**(found mainly in**
**the forearms)**

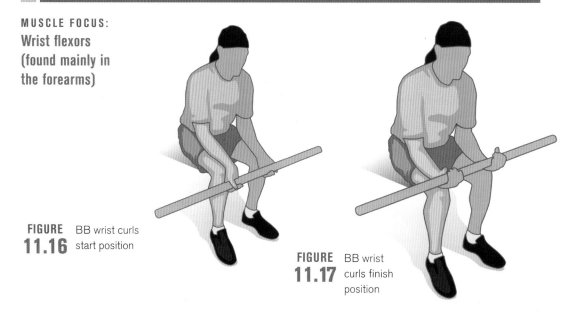

**FIGURE**
**11.16** BB wrist curls start position

**FIGURE**
**11.17** BB wrist curls finish position

The wrists are often overlooked in training for cycling, which is unfortunate because the first muscles that have to work to hold you in position on the bike are in your hands and forearms. If you have ever experienced numbness in your hands, this exercise will help by training the wrists to stay in a stronger position that allows better blood flow.

Holding a barbell with both hands, sit on the end of an exercise bench or a chair. Place your feet about 1 foot apart and lay your forearms on top of your thighs so only your hands hang off past your knees. Adjust your hands so that they are as far apart as your knees are and your palms are facing up. Let your wrists relax and bend down toward the ground, but keep a firm grip on the barbell (Figure 11.16).

Curl your wrists up as far as you can, pulling with both hands at the same time. Keep your forearms firmly planted on your thighs during the movement (Figure 11.17). Let your wrists return to the start position and repeat until your sets are complete.

# 12

# Lower-Body Exercises
# for Cycling

**It doesn't matter how** light and aerodynamic your bike is if your body doesn't have the muscle to propel it forward. Pedaling is a very unusual motor pattern because opposite sides of the body are using opposing muscle groups simultaneously. While one leg is pushing down on the pedal, the other is pulling up. So your glutes, quadriceps, and calf muscles are working on one side, while the hamstrings, hip flexors, and dorsiflexors (front of the lower leg) are working on the other side. This unique motor pattern requires equally unique exercises.

Most lower-body exercises work both legs at the same time, using the same muscles on each leg, so they aren't cycling-specific enough for your needs. The exercises in this chapter were all designed to mimic part of the cycling movement 1 leg at a time. It will take longer to finish each of these exercises because you will have to do twice as many sets (3 sets × 2 legs = 6 sets), so account for the extra time when planning your workouts.

**MUSCLE FOCUS:**
**Quadriceps,**
**glutes, and calves**

**FIGURE 12.2** Walking lunge mid-step position

**FIGURE 12.1** Walking lunge start/finish position

The walking lunge allows you to focus on the pushing part of your cycling stroke. This exercise puts the leg in almost the same position as when you are on the bike and requires you to achieve full extension to get back to the start position. In addition, it alternates left and right legs, just as cycling does.

Find an area like a hallway or gymnasium where you have a clear path. Start by standing with your feet slightly apart, holding a dumbbell in each hand, arms at your sides (Figure 12.1). Take a large step forward with 1 foot. As your foot lands, bend both knees to absorb the impact. Your back knee should move toward the floor but not quite touch it (Figure 12.2). (Touching your knee to the floor puts most of your body weight on one kneecap, which is not a good idea.) The dumbbells should stay at your sides. Once your knee almost touches the floor, push up with both legs, bringing your back foot forward to meet your front foot. Now step forward with your other foot, and continue taking lunging steps until you have completed your set.

**MUSCLE FOCUS:**
**Quadriceps,
glutes, and calves**

The step-up also focuses on the push stroke, but now you have to lift your entire body weight up against the force of gravity. In addition, because you are standing upright and not bent over as you would be on the bike, the quadriceps have to work more, making them even stronger. For this exercise, you can use any height step you want, but about knee height is ideal. You can also check the proper height by putting 1 foot on top of the step and checking to see if the upper leg is nearly parallel to the floor. A step that puts your knee higher than your hip when your foot is on it is too tall and could cause injury to your knee; a shorter step will be too easy.

Stand about 6 to 12 inches from the step. (Standing too far away will cause you to use forward momentum to get up on the step.) Holding a dumbbell in each hand with your arms at your sides, place

**FIGURE 12.3** Step-up proper step height

**FIGURE 12.4** Step-up start position

**FIGURE 12.5** Step-up finish position

your right foot on top of the step, making sure your entire foot is on the step so your heel is not hanging off the edge (Figure 12.3).

Transfer all your body weight onto the right leg and use the muscles in that leg to push yourself up on top of the step (Figure 12.4). It will be temping to use your left leg, especially your calf muscles, to help push you up, but that diminishes the effectiveness of this exercise. Your goal is to have the left foot leave the ground flat-footed (the heel and toes leave the ground at the same time). Once both feet are on top of the step (Figure 12.5), step down with the right leg, keeping the left leg on the step. Now complete a rep by pushing up with the left leg. Alternate, stepping down and pushing up with each leg, until your set is complete.

## ONE-LEG SQUAT

**MUSCLE FOCUS:**
**Quadriceps,**
**glutes, and calves**

**FIGURE**
**12.6**
One-leg squat
start position

The one-leg squat is a very difficult exercise that provides amazing results once you get the hang of it. The depth of the squat is more than you will see on your bike, but it allows the muscles to be stronger and better able to handle the bike range of motion.

Stand next to an exercise machine, doorway, or something you can hold on to with one hand. Standing on 1 foot, lift the other leg out in front and hold it (Figure 12.6). Slowly bend the hip and knee of your

**FIGURE 12.7** One-leg squat finish position

support leg, lowering yourself toward the floor. As you descend, keep holding the other leg off the floor, and let your free arm travel up in front of you for balance (Figure 12.7). Go down as far as you can, or until your support thigh is parallel to the floor. Now push back up with that leg until you are standing again. Repeat until your set is complete, then switch legs to do another set.

**MUSCLE FOCUS:**
**Hip flexors,**
**hamstrings, and**
**dorsiflexors**

This is 1 of only a few exercises that train the recovery portion of the bike stroke. Using the low-pulley machine to mimic having your foot clipped to your bike lets you work the muscles that pull the pedal back to the top of the stroke.

Lie on your back in front of a low-pulley machine, feet toward the machine. You may prop yourself up on your elbows. Hook the ankle strap over the toes of 1 foot far enough so that it won't slip off (Figure 12.8). Make sure there isn't any slack in the cable in this position. Pull back with your toes to make the weight stack rise a little. Keeping your toes pointed up and back, pull your knee toward your chest (Figure 12.9). The other leg should remain on the floor. Slowly return your leg to the start position and repeat until your set is done; then switch legs to do another set.

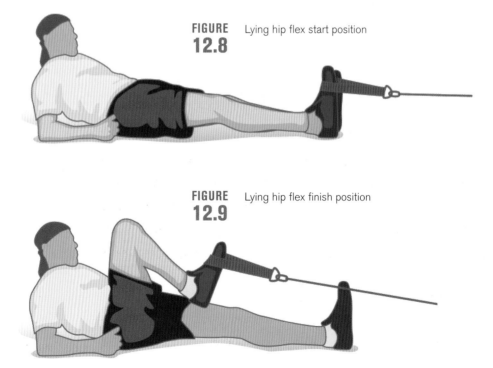

**FIGURE** Lying hip flex start position
**12.8**

**FIGURE** Lying hip flex finish position
**12.9**

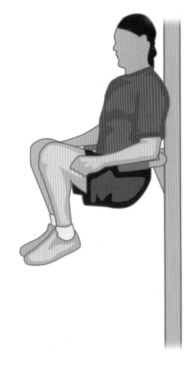

**MUSCLE FOCUS:**
**Hip flexors and hamstrings**

**FIGURE** Knee raise start position
**12.10**

**FIGURE** Knee raise finish position
**12.11**

Knee raises also work the muscle required for pulling your foot back to the top of the stroke, but instead of using a weight stack, you will be lifting your own body weight. Knee raises have often been considered an abdominal exercise, which they are not. Simply put, in order for the abdominals to work, the spine has to flex, because that's what the abdominals are designed to do. There is no spinal flexion during a knee raise, so there is no abdominal action.

There are specific exercise benches made for this exercise, or you can use the arms of a dip machine or straps that allow you to hang from your arms. Position yourself on the equipment so that you are supported by your arms and your legs hang freely off the ground (Figure 12.10).

Pull both knees toward your chest as high as you can (Figure 12.11). Slowly allow them to return toward the ground, and as soon as your legs are straight, lift them again. As a variation, you can alternate lifting 1 leg at a time, in a cycling-type movement (1 leg is coming up while the other is going down). You can add ankle weights to make this exercise more difficult. Complete 15 to 25 reps per set.

## SINGLE-CALF RAISE

**MUSCLE FOCUS:**
**Calves**

The single-calf raise is more specific for cycling because while 1 leg is pushing, the other is pulling, so only 1 side of your body is using your calf muscles at a time. You can do this exercise standing on the floor, but it is more effective to stand on the edge of a step, curb, aerobics bench, or even a board.

Stand with the balls of your feet on the edge of the step so your heels are hanging off the back. Pick up 1 leg and place that foot behind the knee of the other leg (Figure 12.12). Hold on to something to help with balance. Let your support heel drop as far as you can.

**FIGURE**
**12.12**    Single-calf raise start position

Push up on the ball of your foot as high as you can (Figure 12.13). Slowly return to the start position and repeat until the set is complete. Now switch feet to do another set.

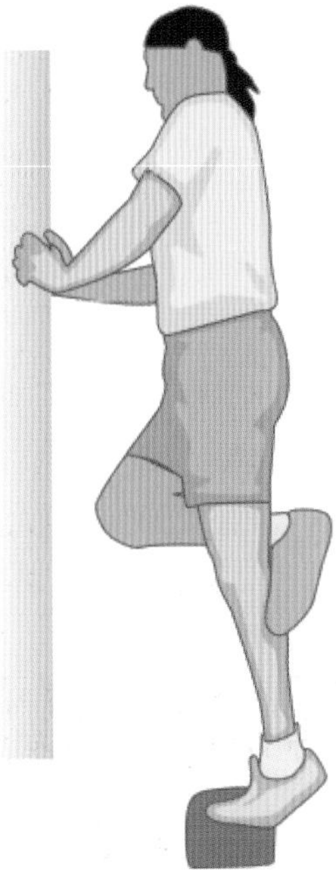

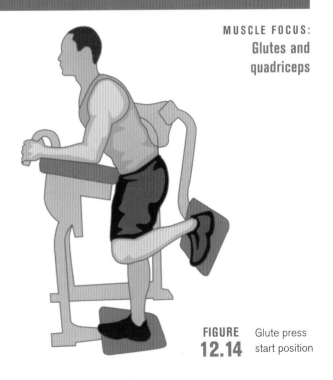

**FIGURE 12.13** Single-calf raise finish position

## GLUTE PRESS

The glute press is similar to the walking lunge and step-up, except that now you can add quite a bit of weight to the movement, so the results happen faster.

Using a glute press or glute extension machine, start by adjusting the machine's elbow or chest pad to a comfortable position that supports your upper body. Place 1 foot on the platform so that it is completely flat and none of your foot hangs off the edge (Figure 12.14). Push back on the platform with the other foot as far as possible (Figure 12.15).

**MUSCLE FOCUS: Glutes and quadriceps**

**FIGURE 12.14** Glute press start position

**FIGURE 12.15** Glute press finish position

Because of the design of these machines, you may not be able to completely extend your leg, so just push as far as you can. Slowly lower the platform back to the start position, but stop just before the weight comes to a rest. Complete another rep until your set is done, then switch legs to do another set.

## SINGLE-LEG EXTENSION

**MUSCLE FOCUS:**
**Quadriceps**

The single-leg extension is cycling-specific because only 1 leg is extending at a time. Just as with the regular leg extension exercise, if you have knee problems, it is better to skip this exercise, but if your knees are healthy, you should be fine.

Sit down on a leg extension machine and adjust the seat back so that your knees line up with the machine's pivot point. The pivot point is always evident (or look at the machine's instruction card) and is usually at the edge of the seat. If your knees are too far for-

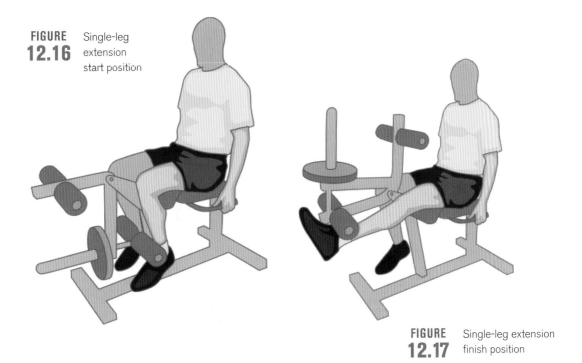

**FIGURE 12.16** Single-leg extension start position

**FIGURE 12.17** Single-leg extension finish position

ward, there will be a lot of strain on them at the start of the exercise. Place your feet behind the footpad and adjust it so the pad rests just above your feet, on your shins (Figure 12.16). (Some machines adjust themselves, so you may not have to do this.) If you can adjust how far under the seat the leg pad is, move it so that you start with your knees bent at about a 90-degree angle. Too much angle at the start can cause knee pain, especially if you have had a knee injury before. If your knees hurt at all during this exercise, skip it and use another exercise instead.

Hold on to the handles and straighten out 1 leg as far as possible (Figure 12.17). Keep the other leg in place, hanging down in a relaxed position. Slowly lower your leg back down to a point just before the weight stack comes to a rest, then repeat until your set is complete. Now do a set with the other leg. Continue alternating legs until all your sets are done.

**MUSCLE FOCUS:**
**Hamstrings**

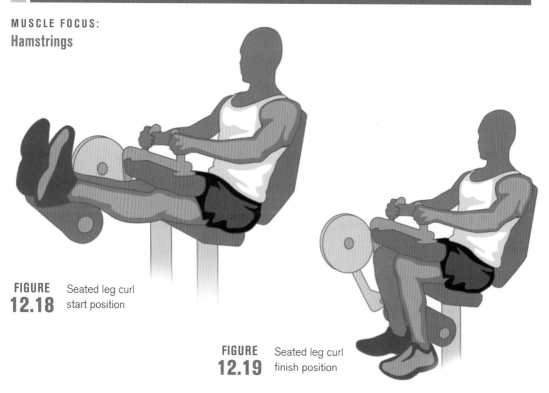

**FIGURE**
**12.18**   Seated leg curl start position

**FIGURE**
**12.19**   Seated leg curl finish position

The seated leg curl is more specific for cycling than the lying leg curl because it places your hips in the flexed position they are in while you are riding your bike. This allows your hamstrings to start in a slightly stretched position, as occurs while cycling.

Sit on the seated leg curl machine and adjust the seat back so your knees line up with the machine's pivot point. The seat is usually quite short on these machines and may stop about halfway to your knees, so be sure to identify the proper pivot point. Put your feet and legs on top of the leg pad (Figure 12.18). Adjust the leg pad so it is in contact with your Achilles tendon and not pushing on your feet. Some machines automatically adjust the footpad, so you may not have to. Lower the thigh pad down until it makes contact and is snug against your thighs. If your knees rise during the exercise, you will have to snug this pad down some more.

Hold on to the hand grips and bend your knees, pulling your feet down and under the seat as far as you can (Figure 12.19). At the end of the pull, give an extra squeeze to go a little farther. Slowly straighten your legs back out until the weights almost touch, then start another rep. Continue reps until your set is complete.

# 13

# Upper-Body Exercises
# for Running

There is an old saying among track coaches that you can run only as fast as you can move your arms. This sounds odd, but the arms and legs move together while you are running. The pumping of your arms acts as a counterbalance to your legs to help rotate your hips and torso. Ever try running with your arms down at your sides? You can't move very fast, and it feels very odd.

Over long distances your upper body can become tired, so the more strength and muscular endurance it has, the better. Also, the up-and-down motion of running causes your shoulders to "bounce," which must be stabilized to prevent injury. Finally, keeping those arms pumping takes muscle. The elbows are bent, which requires the biceps muscles to work, and the entire arm moves forward and back, requiring the shoulders, chest, and back muscles to work.

The upper-body muscles covered in this chapter include the biceps, which keep the elbows bent; the shoulders, which move the arms fore and aft; and the pecs, lats, trapezius, and rhomboids, which stabilize the shoulder movements.

**MUSCLE FOCUS:**
**Biceps**

**FIGURE 13.1** Hammer curl start position

**FIGURE 13.2** Hammer curl finish position

The hammer curl is more specific for running than the DB curl in Chapter 9 because it places the hands in a neutral position, just as they are while you are running and holding your elbows bent. The neutral hand position changes the emphasis of the exercise from the biceps brachii muscle to the brachioradialis muscle (both help bend the elbow), which is used more when you hold your arms in a bent position while running.

Stand with your feet shoulder width apart, 1 foot slightly in front of the other. Hold a dumbbell in each hand, arms straight and relaxed at your sides, palms facing your thighs (Figure 13.1).

Keeping 1 arm at rest, with the other arm pull the dumbbell up to your shoulder by bending your elbow (Figure 13.2). Keep your elbow at your side when you lift the dumbbell—the only part of your arm that should be moving is the forearm and hand. Slowly let the dumbbell back down to the start position, completely straightening the arm, then repeat with the other arm. Alternate left and right curls until your set is complete.

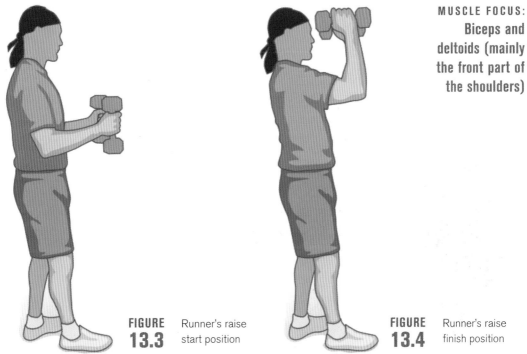

**MUSCLE FOCUS:**
**Biceps and**
**deltoids (mainly**
**the front part of**
**the shoulders)**

**FIGURE 13.3** Runner's raise start position

**FIGURE 13.4** Runner's raise finish position

The runner's raise trains the biceps and shoulders to keep your hands up by your sides during a long run. The alternative is that your arms will slowly hang down, reducing your running efficiency.

Stand with your feet apart, 1 foot slightly in front of the other 1. Hold a dumbbell in each hand. Keeping your elbows at your sides, bend your arms to bring the dumbbells up in front of you, until your arms are at a 90-degree angle (Figure 13.3). (This is basically half of a hammer curl.)

Keeping the dumbbells in this position, lift your elbows forward and up until they are pointing straight out in front of you (Figure 13.4). The dumbbells should have moved toward your head. Slowly lower your arms until your elbows come back to your sides (the dumbbells are still being held up), and repeat until your set is complete.

**MUSCLE FOCUS:**
**Trapezius, deltoids**
**(mainly the top**
**of the shoulders),**
**and biceps**

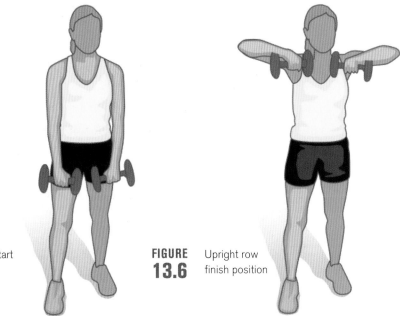

**FIGURE 13.5** Upright row start position

**FIGURE 13.6** Upright row finish position

The upright row also assists in making the shoulders stronger, and with the trapezius prevents your shoulders from bouncing during your run, which can cause fatigue and injury.

Hold a dumbbell in each hand with your arms straight down in front of you and your palms facing the front of your legs (Figure 13.5). Stand with your feet slightly apart.

Lift the dumbbells up to your chin by bending your elbows and pulling the dumbbells straight up the front of your torso (Figure 13.6). Your elbows should end up pointed out to your sides or slightly up. The key is to keep the dumbbells really close to your body at all times and your elbows above your wrists at all times. If you pretend there are strings attached to your elbows that are being pulled from above, the motion will be very smooth. Slowly lower the dumbbells back to the start position and repeat to finish your set.

**MUSCLE FOCUS:**
**Trapezius**

Shrugs help keep your shoulders high and able to hold the weight of your arms without bouncing.

Hold a dumbbell in each hand with your palms facing your thighs and your arms hanging down straight at your sides (Figure 13.7). Stand with your feet together. Let your shoulders sag, allowing the weight of the dumbbells to pull them down. Keeping your arms straight, lift your shoulders up toward your ears, effectively shrugging your shoulders (Figure 13.8). Do not move your shoulders forward or backward or rotate them in a circle—keep your shoulders aligned over your elbows and wrists. Slowly lower them back into the sagging start position and repeat until your set is done.

**FIGURE 13.7** Shrugs start position

**FIGURE 13.8** Shrugs finish position

## RETRACTION

**MUSCLE FOCUS:**
Lats, trapezius, and deltoids (mainly the back of the shoulders)

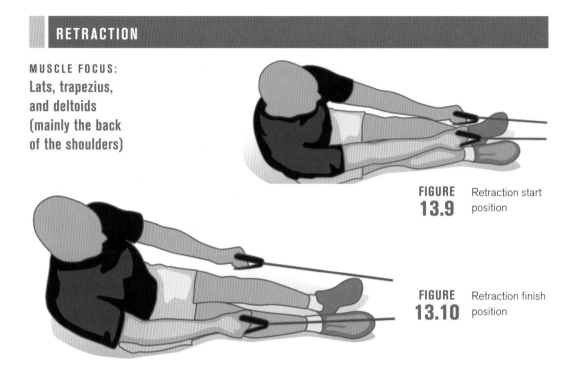

**FIGURE 13.9** Retraction start position

**FIGURE 13.10** Retraction finish position

If you have ever felt your upper back become fatigued during a run or found yourself needing to stretch your shoulders while running, this exercise will help. Retraction also helps keep your torso upright and prevents slouching.

Attach your resistance tubing to the door anchor or wrap it around a pole a couple of feet off the floor. Sit down on the floor facing the anchor. Hold 1 handle in each hand with your arms straight out in front of you (Figure 13.9). Scoot back until the tubing is pulling you forward. Let your shoulders relax so that the tubing is pulling your shoulders forward and your back is rounded.

Keeping your body still and your arms straight, pull your shoulders back while pushing your chest out (Figure 13.10). Your shoulder blades should squeeze back together, and your chest should rise out and up in front of you. This is a small movement, but important for the trapezius muscle.

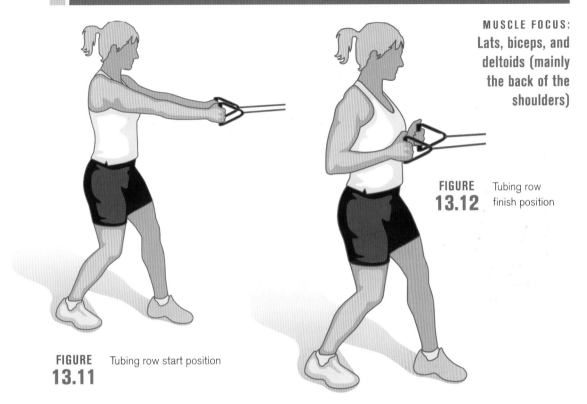

MUSCLE FOCUS:
**Lats, biceps, and deltoids (mainly the back of the shoulders)**

**FIGURE 13.12** Tubing row finish position

**FIGURE 13.11** Tubing row start position

The tubing row will teach you to pull your arms up tight against your body, improving efficiency and aerodynamics, while also strengthening your shoulders and back.

Attach your resistance tubing to the door anchor or wrap it around a pole at shoulder height. Hold 1 handle in each hand. Facing the anchor, hold your arms straight out in front of you, palms facing together, and step back until the tubing is pulling you forward Figure 13.11). Stand with your feet apart and one foot in front of the other to prevent yourself from being pulled forward. Keep your body upright and your back straight.

Pull back on the tubing with both hands, trying to bring your hands all the way to the sides of your body (Figure 13.12). In this position, your arms and hands should be in approximately the same position as they are when you run. Slowly let your arms back out until they are straight again. If there isn't enough resistance, step back a little farther to make the tubing tighter. Repeat until your set is complete.

## LATERAL RAISE

**MUSCLE FOCUS:**
**Trapezius and deltoids (mainly the top middle part of the shoulders)**

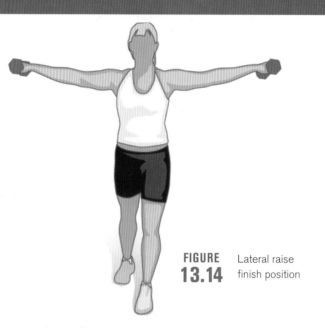

**FIGURE 13.14** Lateral raise finish position

**FIGURE 13.13** Lateral raise start position

You don't often raise your arms out to your sides while running, but training the muscles in this way will help stabilize your shoulders and prevent fatigue.

Stand with your feet apart, 1 foot slightly behind the other for balance. Hold a dumbbell in each hand against the outside of your thighs, palms facing your legs (Figure 13.13). Keeping your arms straight or just slightly bent at the elbow, lift both arms out to your sides until the dumbbells are at shoulder height (Figure 13.14). Slowly lower them back to your sides—don't let them drop quickly. Repeat until your set is finished.

# 14

# Lower-Body Exercises for Running

By the time you get to the run portion of a triathlon, your legs have done a lot of work and are probably starting to fatigue. Fortunately, strength training can give you the extra push you need to keep moving in the late stages of a race by ensuring you have enough muscle strength and endurance.

During the run, your legs are working in opposing directions. While 1 leg is moving back to provide propulsion, the other leg is recovering from the stride and moving forward to start the next stride. This is all done through a very complex motor pattern and the coordination of several muscles. The glutes, quadriceps, hamstrings, and calves are all large muscle groups, so it is important to work each of them in turn, as well as all together. Although there is disagreement about which lower-body muscle group is most important during a run, here we assume they are all equally important and should be worked accordingly—after all, if you take away any 1 muscle group, the rest will suffer.

The running stride is divided into 2 parts, which use different lower-body muscles: the push and the recovery. The push is what propels you forward; it begins when your foot hits the ground in front of you and ends when you lift your foot off the ground to start the recovery. The recovery begins when your foot leaves the ground, continues as it travels back in front of you, and ends when your heel hits the ground to start the next push. The muscles involved in the push include the glutes for hip extension, the hamstrings for hip extension and knee flexion, and the calves for plantarflexion (pushing off). The muscles involved in the recovery include the hip flexors to bring the thigh forward again, the quadriceps to extend the knee, and the shin muscles for dorsiflexion (lifting the toes so you can land heel first).

## SQUAT

**MUSCLE FOCUS:
Glutes, quads,
hamstrings,
and calves**

Although you do not bend your hips and knees as far while running as during the squat, the increased range of motion of this exercise gives the leg muscles a large buffer of strength for the push that propels you forward. The squat is 1 of the greatest exercises for the lower body, but also 1 of the most dangerous. It should always be performed inside a squat cage for maximum safety. The squat cage has 2 upright bars that hold the barbell in place while you load the bar with weight and a pair of safety catch bars that should be used in case you can't get back up from the low position. Adjust the catch bars so they are just below the level the barbell will reach at the lowest squat level.

With the barbell resting on the cage, duck under it and position yourself so it rests across the top of your shoulders, just below your neck. If the bar is uncomfortable, wrap it with a towel for extra padding. Stand up with the barbell, take a small step back, and position your feet shoulder width apart, toes slightly turned out (Figures 14.1 and 14.2).

**FIGURE 14.1**  Squat start/finish position rear view

**FIGURE 14.2**  Squat start position side view

**FIGURE 14.3**  Squat midpoint position rear view

**FIGURE 14.4**  Squat midpoint position side view

Inhale deeply and hold your breath as you descend. Holding your breath creates intra-abdominal pressure, which helps to support your lumbar spine during the descent. Keeping your back straight, bend your knees and hips simultaneously to begin the descent. As you squat, move your hips out behind you and your shoulders forward (Figures 14.3 and 14.4). Be sure to keep the barbell directly over your feet during the entire movement. Squat until your thighs are parallel to the floor (Figure 14.4)—any less is a partial squat and is less effective. Exhale as you push your feet into the floor and stand back up. As you stand, be sure to lift your hips and shoulders at the same time, not 1 then the other. Repeat until your set is complete.

## CABLE HIP FLEX

**MUSCLE FOCUS:**
**Hip flexors and quadriceps**

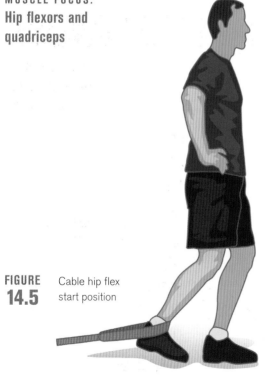

**FIGURE 14.5** Cable hip flex start position

You don't run just by pushing forward; your legs also have to move back in front of you for the next step. When this occurs, your leg moves only through air, so there is no resistance, but the muscles still have to move the weight of your leg. The cable hip flex exercise works the hip flexors and quadriceps muscles responsible for the recovery.

Attach the ankle strap of a low-pulley machine to 1 leg. You can also put your toes through a single handle strap instead of using the ankle strap. Stand facing away from the machine and step away until there is resistance on the cable and the attached leg is slightly behind you (Figure 14.5). Hold on to something for balance if you need to.

Keeping your leg straight and your toes pointed up, slowly raise your leg out in front of you as high as you can (Figure 14.6). Don't try to kick or use momentum to get your leg any higher. Slowly lower your leg back to the start position, repeat until your set is done, then switch legs.

**FIGURE 14.6** Cable hip flex finish position

## SPLIT SQUAT

The split squat is similar to the regular squat, but you use body weight, not a barbell. The range of motion for each leg is greater than you will encounter during running, but it teaches your legs to move the weight of your body, with each leg using different muscles to do so.

Holding a dumbbell in each hand with your palms facing your thighs, stand straight with your feet together. Take a big step forward with 1 leg (Figure 14.7). Bend both knees so that your back knee moves toward the floor

**MUSCLE FOCUS:**
**Quadriceps, hamstrings, calves, and glutes**

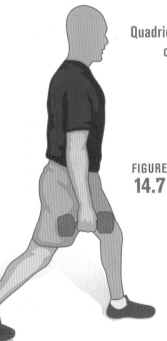

**FIGURE 14.7** Split squat start position

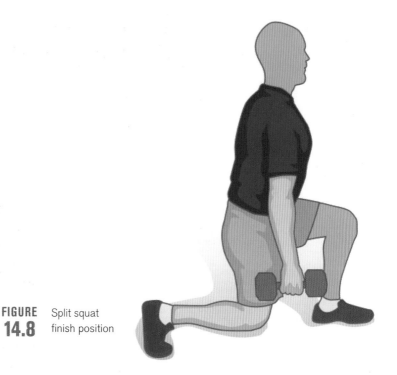

**FIGURE 14.8** Split squat finish position

and your front knee moves toward your toes. Your knee should move past your toes. The deeper bend at the knee will provide greater results from this exercise. (However, if you have had a posterior cruciate ligament injury, you should step out farther to keep your knees behind your toes.)

Keep your torso upright and straight; do not lean forward. Stop when your back knee is about an inch from the floor (Figure 14.8). Push against the floor with both feet to rise back up to the start position. The dumbbells should remain hanging at your sides the entire time. Repeat until your set is done, then switch so the other leg is in front, and do another set.

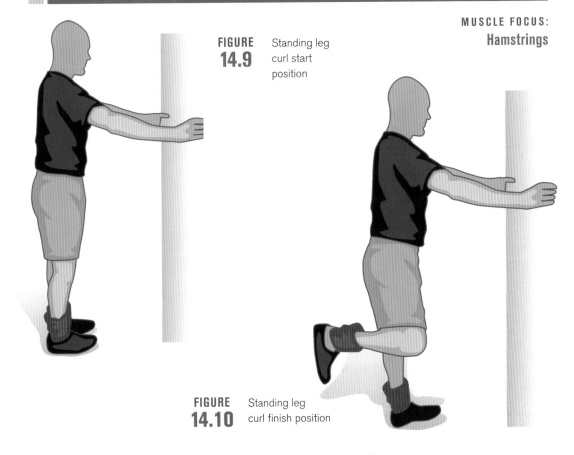

**MUSCLE FOCUS:**
**Hamstrings**

**FIGURE 14.9** Standing leg curl start position

**FIGURE 14.10** Standing leg curl finish position

The standing leg curl is the most specific hamstring exercise for running because it places you in the same position you are in while running: standing up.

Attach an ankle weight to each leg. If you need more resistance, wrap a second ankle weight over the first. Stand facing something you can hold on to for balance. Keep your feet about 1 foot apart (Figure 14.9).

Lift the toes of 1 foot off the floor, then bend your knee to bring that foot up behind you (Figure 14.10). Pretend you are trying to kick yourself in the buttocks, but not hard. As you lift the foot, do not lean forward; keep your torso upright and straight. Try hard to lift the foot as high as you can in a controlled manner, letting your knee move behind you to really get it up there. Lower the foot back to the floor and repeat until the set is done. Switch to the other leg and do another set.

## SINGLE-LEG LYING CURL

**MUSCLE FOCUS:**
**Hamstrings**

**FIGURE 14.11** Single-leg lying curl start position

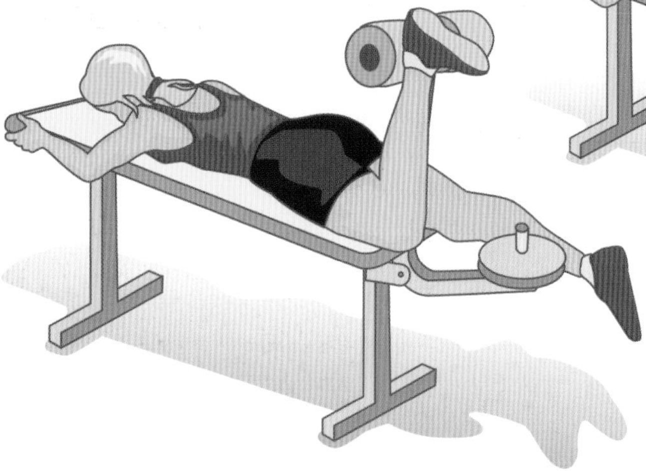

**FIGURE 14.12** Single-leg lying curl finish position

The single-leg lying curl makes each leg work on its own and allows you to use more weight, so you can get more individualized results and improve your running.

Find the pivot point of the lying leg curl machine, usually at the edge of the padding. Stand at the end of the bench with your knees right against the padding and lie down on your front, holding on to the handles (Figure 14.11). Your kneecaps should hang off the end of the bench and be lined up with the machine pivot point. (Some machines have pads for your elbows to rest on; others have a flat bench to rest your chest and head on.) Your feet should be underneath the leg pad. Some machines adjust this automatically, but if not, adjust it so it is in contact with the back of your shins (on your Achilles tendon) and is not pushing on your foot.

Keeping 1 leg relaxed and in the start position, pull the leg pad as far up as you can with the other leg (Figure 14.12). The goal is to get the pad all the way to your buttocks. The farther you can curl your leg, the more you will get out of this exercise. Slowly lower the leg, then repeat until your set is complete. Switch legs and do another set.

## CABLE TOE RAISE

The cable toe raise focuses on the muscles in the front of your shins, which are responsible for lifting your toes during the recovery stride. If these muscles are weak, you will drag your toes on the ground and have a hard time landing heel first.

**MUSCLE FOCUS:
Dorsiflexors
(shin muscles)**

Sit on the floor facing a low-pulley machine. Place the toes of 1 foot through a single handle strap attached to the cable. Scoot yourself back until the cable is pulling your toes toward the machine (Figure 14.13). You can rest on your elbows or your hands.

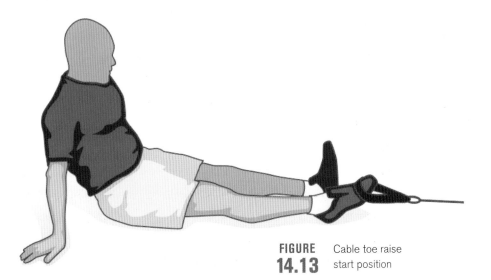

**FIGURE
14.13**   Cable toe raise start position

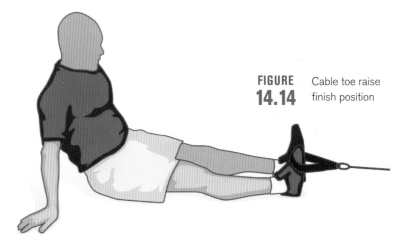

**FIGURE**
**14.14**
Cable toe raise
finish position

Pull your toes toward you as far as you can, then slowly let them
back toward the machine (Figure 14.14). Complete all your reps on
that foot, then switch and do a set on the other foot.

## SEATED TOE RAISE

**MUSCLE FOCUS:**
**Dorsiflexors**

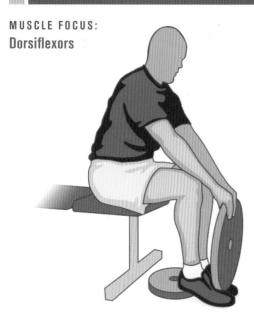

**FIGURE**
**14.15**
Seated toe raise
start position

The seated toe raise focuses on the front of the
shins, but both feet are working together, and
with the knees bent, the body has to work harder
to move a light weight.

Place a 25- to 45-pound weight plate on the
floor in front of a chair or bench. Sitting on the
edge of the chair or bench, move the plate so
that your heels are on the edge of the plate and
your toes hang off the end. Put your feet together and keep your heels directly under your
knees so your toes are in front of your knees.
Place another weight plate on your toes and
hold it there with both hands. Allow your toes
to drop to the floor and relax (Figure 14.15).

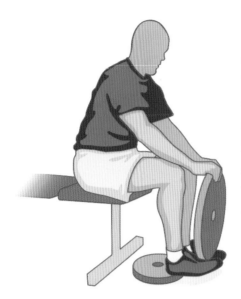

Lift the toes of both feet as high as you can, lifting the weight plate with your toes (Figure 14.16). You can rock back on your heels, but don't move your upper body or legs; only your feet and ankles should move. Lower your toes back to the floor and repeat until the set is complete.

**FIGURE 14.16** Seated toe raise finish position

## LEG PRESS

**MUSCLE FOCUS:
Glutes, quadriceps,
hamstrings, and calves**

**FIGURE 14.17** Leg press start position

The leg press is really just a squat in a seated position. The benefit is that there is no weight on your shoulders; it moves through your hips instead, so it is safer.

Sit in a leg press machine with your feet on the platform, spaced slightly wider than shoulder width apart, with your toes pointed out slightly. Be sure to keep your feet completely on the platform; don't let your heels hang off the bottom. Adjust the seat until your knees are bent at about 90 degrees. An angle greater than 90 degrees will put too much strain on the knees, whereas an angle of less than 90 degrees will decrease the effectiveness of the exercise. If the machine allows you to adjust the backrest, make it comfortable. Place your hands on the handles down at your sides (Figure 14.17).

Push against the platform with both feet at the same time. When you push, put equal pressure on your heels and the balls of your feet. Don't allow the focus to be on your toes; that would make this a calf exercise only. Push until your legs are not quite straight (Figure 14.18). Do not lock your knees! Slowly bend your legs, letting the platform move back toward you. When the weights almost touch, repeat until your set is finished.

**FIGURE**
**14.18** Leg press finish position

# Needs Analysis Visual Index

Here are some stretches and exercises that target common problem or growth areas for triathletes. After determining which symptom(s) you are experiencing, add all the stretches listed for that symptom to your program, and then choose up to 3 of the provided exercises. If you are training for multiple events or addressing multiple symptoms, it's important that you limit yourself to 3 exercises per muscle group.

## SWIMMING

SYMPTOM: you have to rest your legs periodically and rely more on your arms
CAUSE: relatively weak lower body
SOLUTION: strengthen quads, glutes, hips

| | hip diagonals stretch | pp. 61–62 |
|---|---|---|
| | hip side skate stretch | p. 62 |

| | | |
|---|---|---|
| | quad step stretch | pp. 62–63 |
| | cable lateral lift (gluteus medius) | pp. 118–119 |
| | inclined Superman (gluteus maximus, hamstrings) | p. 119 |
| | leg extension (quadriceps) | pp. 120–121 |
| | cable hip extension (gluteus maximus, hamstrings) | p. 122 |
| | lying leg curl (hamstrings) | pp. 124–125 |

**SYMPTOM:** you have to kick harder at times to let your arms rest
**CAUSE:** relatively weak upper body
**SOLUTION:** strengthen shoulders, arms, back

| | | |
|---|---|---|
| | biceps twisters stretch | p. 57 |

| | | |
|---|---|---|
| | triceps pretzel stretch | p. 58 |
| | shoulder cross-pull stretch | p. 58 |
| | shoulder turnaround stretch | p. 59 |
| | upper-back pole-pull stretch | p. 61 |
| | slam dunk (lats, deltoids, triceps) | pp. 105–106 |
| | dumbbell shoulder press (deltoids, triceps) | pp. 109–110 |
| | triceps push-down (triceps) | p. 111 |
| | dumbbell curl (biceps) | pp. 115–116 |

| | | |
|---|---|---|
| **SYMPTOM:** your body roll decreases the farther or longer you swim<br>**CAUSE:** core muscles are tiring<br>**SOLUTION:** add core exercises that work on rotation | | |
| | combination crunch | p. 92 |
| | Russian ball twist | pp. 97–98 |
| | moguls | pp. 99–100 |
| | diagonal wood chop | pp. 100–101 |
| | twisting punch | pp. 101–102 |
| **SYMPTOM:** one leg gets more tired than the other<br>**CAUSE:** muscular imbalance in legs<br>**SOLUTION:** incorporate more single-leg exercises | | |
| | cable hip extension (gluteus maximus, hamstrings) | p. 122 |
| | cable lateral cross (adductors) | p. 123 |

SYMPTOM: one arm or shoulders get more tired than the other
CAUSE: muscular imbalance in arms and/or shoulder
SOLUTION: incorporate more single-arm exercises

| | | |
|---|---|---|
| | one-arm throw (lats, deltoids) | pp. 104–105 |
| | tubing stroke (lats, deltoids, biceps, triceps) | pp. 108–109 |
| | tubing kickback (triceps) | pp. 112–113 |

SYMPTOM: you sometimes have to increase your stroke rate in order to maintain the same speed
CAUSE: not enough muscular endurance and weak upper body
SOLUTION: increase reps and number of upper-body exercises

| | | |
|---|---|---|
| | biceps twisters stretch | p. 57 |
| | triceps pretzel stretch | p. 58 |
| | shoulder cross-pull stretch | p. 58 |
| | shoulder turnaround stretch | p. 59 |
| | chest bow stretch | p. 59 |

**Swimming** Increase reps and number of upper-body exercises, continued

| | | |
|---|---|---|
| | slam dunk (lats, deltoids, triceps) | pp. 105–106 |
| | bridging pullover (lats, deltoids) | pp. 106–107 |
| | tubing stroke (lats, deltoids, biceps, triceps) | pp. 108–109 |
| | dips (triceps, deltoids) | pp. 113–114 |
| | seated dips (triceps, deltoids) | pp. 114–115 |
| | dumbbell curl (biceps) | pp. 115–116 |

## CYCLING

**SYMPTOM:** you push harder with one leg or the other
**CAUSE:** muscular imbalance in legs
**SOLUTION: use more weight or repetitions on single-leg exercises for weak side**

| | | |
|---|---|---|
| | walking lunge (quadriceps, glutes, calves) | p. 140 |

**Cycling** Use more weight or repetitions on single-leg exercises for weak side, continued

| | | |
|---|---|---|
| | step-up (quadriceps, glutes, calves) | pp. 141–142 |
| | one-leg squats (quadriceps, glutes, calves) | pp. 142–143 |
| | lying hip flex (hip flexors, hamstrings, dorsiflexors) | p. 144 |
| | glute press (glutes, quadriceps) | pp. 147–148 |
| | single-leg extension (quadriceps) | pp. 148–149 |

**SYMPTOM:** your thighs start to get tired before your hips and glutes
**CAUSE:** weak quadriceps
**SOLUTION:** incorporate more exercises that extend the knee

| | | |
|---|---|---|
| | step-up (quadriceps, glutes, calves) | pp. 141–142 |
| | one-leg squats (quadriceps, glutes, calves) | pp. 142–143 |

**Cycling** Incorporate more exercises that extend the knee, continued

| | | |
|---|---|---|
| | glute press (glutes, quadriceps) | pp. 147–148 |
| | single-leg extension (quadriceps) | pp. 148–149 |

**SYMPTOM:** your heels start to drop below your toes as you push on the pedals
**CAUSE:** weak calf muscles
**SOLUTION:** add more calf raises, step ups, and walking lunges

| | | |
|---|---|---|
| | calf wall-step stretch | p. 63 |
| | walking lunge (quadriceps, glutes, calves) | p. 140 |
| | step-up (quadriceps, glutes, calves) | pp. 141–142 |
| | single-calf raise (calves) | pp. 146–147 |

## Cycling continued

| | | |
|---|---|---|
| **SYMPTOM:** your arms or shoulders become fatigued if you don't use aerobars<br>**CAUSE:** weak shoulders and/or arms<br>**SOLUTION:** strengthen your shoulders and triceps | | |
| | triceps pretzel stretch | p. 58 |
| | shoulder cross-pull stretch | p. 58 |
| | shoulder turnaround stretch | p. 59 |
| | front raise (deltoids) | p. 133 |
| | dumbbell handle push-up (pecs, triceps, deltoids) | pp. 134–135 |
| | dumbbell incline press (pecs, triceps, deltoids) | p. 136 |
| | shoulder dips (trapezius, rhomboids) | p. 137 |

## Cycling continued

| | | |
|---|---|---|
| **SYMPTOM:** your shoulders or upper back become fatigued while using aerobars<br>**CAUSE:** weak shoulders and/or upper back<br>**SOLUTION:** strengthen shoulders and upper back | | |
| | shoulder cross-pull stretch | p. 58 |
| | shoulder turnaround stretch | p. 59 |
| | upper-back pole-pull stretch | p. 61 |
| | protraction (pecs, deltoids) | p. 132 |
| | front raise (deltoids) | p. 133 |
| | dumbbell incline press (pecs, triceps, deltoids) | p. 136 |
| | shoulder dips (trapezius, rhomboids) | p. 137 |

**Cycling** continued

| | | |
|---|---|---|
| SYMPTOM: your back sags instead of staying flat<br>CAUSE: upper and lower back are weak<br>SOLUTION: include more core exercises to strengthen the back | | |
| | chest bow stretch | p. 59 |
| | lower-back leaning tower stretch | p. 60 |
| | pointer (erector spinae, rhomboids, trapezius, lats) | pp. 90–91 |
| | modified bridge (erector spinae, rhomboids) | p. 95 |
| | back bridge (erector spinae, rhomboids) | pp. 96–97 |
| | back extension (erector spinae, rhomboids, trapezius) | pp. 130–131 |

SYMPTOM: you drag your toes
CAUSE: shin muscles are weak
SOLUTION: strengthen shin muscles

| | | |
|---|---|---|
| | cable toe raise (dorsiflexors) | pp. 169–170 |
| | seated toe raise (dorsiflexors) | pp. 170–171 |

SYMPTOM: your hamstrings get tired before your quads
CAUSE: muscle imbalance in thighs
SOLUTION: include more hamstring exercises

| | | |
|---|---|---|
| | hamstring towel-pull stretch | p. 63 |
| | squat (glutes, quads, hamstrings, calves) | pp. 162–163 |
| | split squat (quadriceps, hamstrings, calves, glutes) | pp. 165–166 |

| | | |
|---|---|---|
| | standing leg curl (hamstrings) | pp. 167–168 |
| | single-leg lying curl (hamstrings) | pp. 168–169 |
| | leg press (glutes, quadriceps, hamstrings, calves) | pp. 171–172 |

**SYMPTOM:** your quads get tired before your hamstrings
**CAUSE:** muscle imbalance in thighs
**SOLUTION:** include more quad exercises

| | | |
|---|---|---|
| | quad step stretch | pp. 62–63 |
| | squat (glutes, quads, hamstrings, calves) | pp. 162–163 |
| | cable hip flex (hip flexors, quadriceps) | pp. 164–165 |

| | | |
|---|---|---|
| | split squat (quadriceps, hamstrings, calves, glutes) | pp. 165–166 |
| | leg press (glutes, quadriceps, hamstrings, calves) | pp. 171–172 |

**SYMPTOM:** your arms drop lower during long runs
**CAUSE:** biceps fatigue
**SOLUTION: add more biceps exercises and repetitions**

| | | |
|---|---|---|
| | biceps twisters stretch | p. 57 |
| | hammer curl (biceps) | p. 154 |
| | runner's raise (biceps, deltoids) | p. 155 |
| | upright row (trapezius, deltoids, biceps) | p. 156 |
| | tubing row (lats, biceps, deltoids) | pp. 159–160 |

SYMPTOM: your shoulders get tight or start to hurt
CAUSE: shoulder are bouncing and fatiguing
SOLUTION: focus more on shoulder strength for running

| | | |
|---|---|---|
| | shoulder cross-pull stretch | p. 58 |
| | shoulder turnaround stretch | p. 59 |
| | runner's raise (biceps, deltoids–front) | p. 155 |
| | upright row (trapezius, deltoids-top, biceps) | p. 156 |
| | shrugs (trapezius) | p. 157 |
| | retraction (lats, trapezius, deltoids–back) | p. 158 |
| | tubing row (lats, biceps, deltoids–back) | pp. 159–160 |
| | lateral raise (trapezius, deltoids–top middle) | p. 160 |

| | | |
|---|---|---|
| SYMPTOM: you find yourself leaning forward<br>CAUSE: lower back fatigue<br>SOLUTION: include more upright core exercises | | |
| | abdominal arch | p. 60 |
| | diagonal wood chop | pp. 100–101 |
| | twisting punch | pp. 101–102 |
| SYMPTOM: your strides get shorter as you run longer<br>CAUSE: hip and glute fatigue<br>SOLUTION: increase exercises for hip and range of motion used | | |
| | hip diagonals stretch | pp. 61–62 |
| | hip side skate stretch | p. 62 |
| | quad step stretch | pp. 62–63 |

**Running** Increase exercises for hip and range of motion used, continued

| | | |
|---|---|---|
| | squats (glutes, quads, hamstrings, calves) | pp. 162–163 |
| | cable hip flex (hip flexors, quadriceps) | pp. 164–165 |
| | split squat (quadriceps, hamstrings, calves, glutes) | pp. 165–166 |
| | leg press (glutes, quadriceps, hamstrings, calves) | pp. 171–172 |

# Daily Training Log

Here's a sample Daily Training Log that follows the first microcycle (week 1) of the first mesocycle in Table 7.2 on page 80. Blank logs follow for your own use.

## Sample Daily Training Log

**Date:** December 9
**Goal:** 55% 1RM or medium-weight blue tubing. 3 sets of 15 reps.

| Exercise | Set # | Reps | Weight |
|---|---|---|---|
| Lateral raise<br>1RM = 20 | 1 | 15 | 17.5 |
| | 2 | 14 | 17.5 |
| | 3 | 13 | 17.5 |
| Hammer curl<br>1RM = 35 | 1 | 15 | 20 |
| | 2 | 13 | 20 |
| | 3 | 13 | 20 |
| Squat<br>1RM = 175 | 1 | 15 | 95 |
| | 2 | 14 | 95 |
| | 3 | 12 | 95 |
| Standing leg curl<br>1RM = 75 | 1 | 15 | 40 |
| | 2 | 15 | 40 |
| | 3 | 14 | 40 |
| Runner's raise<br>1RM = 45 | 1 | 15 | 25 |
| | 2 | 14 | 25 |
| | 3 | 12 | 25 |
| Tubing row | 1 | 15 | Blue |
| | 2 | 13 | Blue |
| | 3 | 12 | Blue |

**Notes:** Good workout. Next time, decrease rest on standing leg curl and squat.

## Daily Training Log

**Date:**

**Goal:**

| Exercise | Set # | Reps | Weight |
|----------|-------|------|--------|
|          |       |      |        |
|          |       |      |        |
|          |       |      |        |
|          |       |      |        |
|          |       |      |        |
|          |       |      |        |

**Notes:**

## Daily Training Log

**Date:**

**Goal:**

| Exercise | Set # | Reps | Weight |
|---|---|---|---|
|  |  |  |  |
|  |  |  |  |
|  |  |  |  |
|  |  |  |  |
|  |  |  |  |
|  |  |  |  |

**Notes:**

# About the Author

**DR. PATRICK HAGERMAN,** EdD, FNSCA, CSCS, NSCA-CPT, HFI, is the Director of Sport Skill Development for Quest Personal Training. He has been a professor of exercise and sports science, a university-level strength and conditioning coach, a personal trainer, and an athlete. He is a Fellow of the National Strength and Conditioning Association and a past member of its Board of Directors. In 2002 he won the Personal Trainer of the Year (NSCA) award. He is certified by the NSCA and ACSM; is a USA Triathlon– and USA Weightlifting–certified coach; and has competed in triathlon, cycling, windsurfing, and adventure racing for over 25 years. Dr. Hagerman is assistant editor-in-chief of the *Strength and Conditioning Journal* and the author of four other books. He has written chapters for numerous textbooks, and has published more than 20 articles on strength and conditioning.